Everyday Hopes,
Utopian Dreams

Also by Don Hanlon Johnson

Body, Spirit and Democracy

Body: Recovering Our Sensual Wisdom

Groundworks: Narratives of Embodiment (editor)

Bone, Breath, & Gesture: Practices of Embodiment (editor)

The Body in Psychotherapy: Inquiries in Somatic Psychology
(co-editor)

The Protean Body

EVERYDAY HOPES, UTOPIAN DREAMS

Reflections on American Ideals

DON HANLON JOHNSON

North Atlantic Books
Berkeley, California

Published by
North Atlantic Books
P.O. Box 12327   Cover and book design by Susan Quasha
Berkeley, California 94712   Printed in the United States of America

Everyday Hopes, Utopian Dreams: Reflections on American Ideals is sponsored by the Society for the Study of Native Arts and Sciences, a nonprofit educational corporation whose goals are to develop an educational and crosscultural perspective linking various scientific, social, and artistic fields; to nurture a holistic view of arts, sciences, humanities, and healing; and to publish and distribute literature on the relationship of mind, body, and nature.

North Atlantic Books' publications are available through most bookstores. For further information, call 800-337-2665 or visit our website at www.northatlanticbooks.com. Substantial discounts on bulk quantities are available to corporations, professional associations, and other organizations. For details and discount information, contact our special sales department.

Library of Congress Cataloging-in-Publication Data

Johnson, Don, 1934–
    Everyday hopes, Utopian dreams : reflections on American ideals / Don Hanlon Johnson.
        p. cm.
    Includes bibliographical references.
    ISBN-13: 978-1-55643-599-7 (pbk.)
    ISBN-10: 1-55643-599-1 (pbk.)
    1. Johnson, Don, 1934–Childhood and youth. 2. Johnson, Don, 1934–Family. 3. Sacramento (Calif.)–Biography. 4. Sacramento (Calif.)—Social life and customs–20th century. 5. Sacramento (Calif.)–Social conditions–20th century. 6. United States Social conditions–1980– 7. Social problems–United States. 8. National characteristics, American. 9. Ideals (Philosophy) 10. Social values–United States. I. Title.
    F869.S12J64 2006
    979.4'54053092–dc22
    [B]
                                                    2006018909

1 2 3 4 5 6 7 UNITED 10 09 08 07 06

For Barbara and Tano.
SOURCES OF HOPE

Contents

1

Frayed Hopes

And how far is it from the point where we find ourselves today back to the late eighteenth century, when
the hope that mankind could improve and learn was in-
scribed in handsomely formed letters in our philosophical firmament?

—W. G. SEBALD, "An Attempt at Restitution"[1]

DURING THE 1970s, my father organized into framed montages
hundreds of photos, which he and my mother had stored
over a lifetime in boxes in the basement of the house he
built in Sacramento in 1939, a few blocks from the State Capitol.
He hung them on the walls of his tiny knotty-pine den. Some date
back to the 1880s: formal studio portraits of his mother's family in
Göteberg, Sweden; my grandfather Jul outfitted as a Rough Rider
for the Spanish-American War; Great-Uncle Charley on his horse
herding cattle; Great-Uncle Andy in miner's gear; my mother's
grandmother Lucy with the last of her three husbands; my mother's
parents in love sashaying through Capitol Park in period dress. Poignant photos of my mother as a young girl playing with her friends
in the neighborhood before her mother's early death of breast cancer capture a radiantly happy expression that I was never to see.
My father stands lean and handsome next to his father's model
T. My newlywed parents are shown picnicking with their young
adult friends along the Consumnes River, long before my younger

cousin drowned there. They appear at Seabright on the Monterey Bay, and fishing in the Sierra Nevada before I was born. In later photos, they show signs of having gained a modest purchase on the post-war wealth of California, better-fed and well-dressed on trips to Sun Valley, Maui, Miami, and Scotland. I begin to appear: on my skis at four years old on the old Donner Pass road; playing on the sand at Santa Cruz and wasting away summers among my mother's friends while other boys were playing volleyball and surfing; shouldering my shotgun on hunting trips in the Sutter Buttes when I was in grade school.

On visits, I used to sit quietly in that den awash in Proustian reveries evoked by images of the worlds we came from and where we have arrived, often overcome by a bleak feeling of absence. With the exception of the old studio portraits where our forebears had more neutral expressions, the people in every other photo are smiling, or more probably saying "cheese." Their chronic smiles belie the struggles we had all undergone to carve our lives out of a rough new land. The most authentic smile I have ever come across occurs in a series of four mounted pictures of my father as a baby in his lace baptismal gown, which I found when I was going through musty, long-unopened boxes after he died. His eyes have the familiar bright wit of later pictures, but without the adult veil of anger and bitterness. I imagine that he never hung that picture because it must have been hard for him to contemplate its promise of a joy that he never was able fully to realize.

There are glaring omissions in the record. Photos of my fourteen years in the Catholic religious order of Jesuits once hung in that den: me in my black soutane at our Los Gatos Novitiate, and our philosophy school on a mesa outside Spokane; on outings with Jesuit friends and my parents; in ceremonial priestly vestments at my ordination as a priest in Sacramento's Cathedral. My father removed those from the record of our lives when I left the priesthood the uniformed captain, a forced smile on his face; my mother, erect beside them in formal dress. I cannot imagine him looking long at that overly constructed portrait of elder-travel happiness without a measure of disgust, given that he had always disdained such cultivated ideals in favor of dreams of a more earthy life riding the range as a cattle-rancher, hunting and fishing in the wilderness.

Every time I drive my car into my mother's garage and make the short walk past those pictures into her kitchen, I travel into and out of my family's highly edited version of the American Dream. Unfortunately, like Thomas Kinkade's paintings and Lawrence Welk's music, the cloying smiles reeking of nostalgia and the absence of any traces of the constant challenges of poverty and sickness back in our histories create despair instead of the innocent happiness they are arranged to evoke. A cynicism haunted my father's final years, which took away his ability to appreciate his many solid achievements for my mother and me and for those who worked for him. It now haunts me. In the face of it, I have had to examine the many gaps in the record with the conviction that only a full picture of pain, resentment, hard work, wild desires, and a host of other human expressions might sustain hopes resilient enough to navigate through the blinding ground fogs of personal depression and communal cynicism.

My lifetime pursuits of studying, teaching, and writing have been marked by a characteristically American innocence that has taken root here because of the vast geographical distances that separate our everyday lives from the many other parts of the world that have been visited by constant tragedy during the past century. That innocence allowed me to base my work on the assumption that it is possible in the course of a lifetime to make the world at least a little better, not just the close-to-hand world of family and friends, but the larger world of war, famine, disease, and environmental degradation. In my childhood, I could feel in our home the idealism of Franklin Roosevelt's New Deal, which was giving my family its first chance to emerge from poverty into the security and comfort of the middle class. Catholic teachers stoked that latent excitement about bettering the world. Many of them were fired up by the humane morality of Jesus and the social teachings of the Popes of the last century, which enjoined Catholics to shape a society in which the fruits of work are more equitably distributed, and everyone, no matter how peculiar, is treated at least with justice if not respect. My later education in philosophy, the sciences, and the humanisms of older cultures augmented those earlier teachings with the promise of a world in which sectarian ideologies based on other-worldly ideals would give way to a more tolerant commonweal.

Although I have often had to whittle back the wild utopianisms of my early adulthood in the face of both my own shortcomings and the repetitive tendencies of societies to undercut their own welfare, I was able to hold on to at least a modest hope for human progress as the energizing force of my work. That hope collapsed in the months after 9/11 when our nation took a turn that seemed to be an argument in favor of a deterministic cyclical view of history in which any appearance of progress is merely a short-sighted illusion.

When I woke at six o'clock on 9/11, I lay looking out towards the east beyond our quiet redwood canyon, the sky still gray and a little misty before sunrise, not knowing that if at that very moment my gaze could keep right on going over the Continent I would see the change of our lives just beginning. After tea and a few quiet moments meditating with my wife, sitting on our stairs watching the sun inch up above the redwoods and the bay trees, with the yellow finches and bushtits singing richly, getting ready for their journeys south, I called a friend in New York. It struck me as odd that the lines were all busy. I wondered if the stock market had taken a dramatic turn downward.

On the way home from dropping my son at school, noticing the car clock at 8:01, I turned on the news. Catching it in mid-sentence,

I thought I was hearing a typical exaggeration of a daily accident in some small town in the Midwest. The horror slowly took me over as I drove up our dead-end road. Stunned by the unfolding scenes on television, I decided to take a walk on Diaz Ridge near our home, which travels between Green Gulch canyon and Muir Woods, down to the ocean at Muir Beach. It was balmy and clear, a South Pacific feeling, strangely silent as a result of the suspended air traffic. As I rounded a bend, a bobcat was standing quietly in the middle of the road looking away from me. I stopped and waited a few minutes until it turned and saw me, and ran quickly away. As I was nearing the end of the trail back I luckily noticed that just off the center of the path, in shade cast by the brush, lay a medium-sized rattlesnake. We paused quietly and watched each other and I passed on.

When Pearl Harbor was attacked, I was exactly the same age as my son was on 9/11. My life was never the same. Like everyone else, our outer lives were changed in ways that are well known—the disruptions of World War II itself, the post-war boom, the Cold War, and the residues in world politics. My inner life changed too, from then on haunted by images of killer airplanes swooping down in the middle of the night, furtive submarines landing on the coast to debark soldiers who would attack us in the streets. All in the name of God, Allah, or some utopian ideal. And yet, unlike now, World War II was suffused with a new national purpose, an emergence of a self-enclosed national image into the world community, an idealism of free nations helping each other stand up against old-style imperial tyrannies.

Now, by contrast, we seem to have circled back to the early Middle Ages. Muslims, Christians, and Hindus are once again slaughtering each other and destroying their shared achievements in literature, architecture, and science, with the Jews, Zoroastrians, and other less militant groups crushed in between. Yet worse, because the weapons now available are capable of destruction beyond what anyone might have imagined at Pearl Harbor.

The natural sciences, having matured over four centuries of brilliant investigations of the macroscopic and the microscopic, are being called into question in a manner that brings to mind the arguments of the Roman Inquisition against Galileo. Microbiologists, climatologists, ecological scientists, and many others are characterized by religious dogmatists as representing just another worldview, on equal footing (at best!) with biblical accounts of cosmic origins and the evolution of the natural world.

After a century of witnessing the rapid decline of colonial empires, we find ourselves at the heart of the biggest one in history, employing legally sanctioned torture, the extermination of women and children, and the appropriation of natural resources as reasonable national strategies.

I recalled the jolt to my late 1960s idealism when I read Hannah Arendt's *On Revolution,* in which she argues that revolution, whose meaning is derived from "revolving," changes nothing except that those on the bottom succeed in getting to the top by putting the old rulers on the bottom, while taking on their manner of governance. Progress, in the words of Walter Benjamin and Laurie Anderson, is an angel moving backwards into the future. I found myself calling into question my writing and my teaching, seeing them as an illusory dance in the face of the inevitability of what Freud postulated as an intrinsic death instinct driving us willy-nilly to destroy our best achievements.

Struggling to work myself out of that despondent emotional swamp, I found myself going back to the earliest situations within which my own idealism was shaped. There, perhaps, would be clues to what is enduring in the midst of what is illusory.

While I was working on this text, I was driving with my young son Tano and two of his friends, Jason and Ian, in the back seat.

Jason said, "Don, if you had three wishes for anything, what would they be?" As Tano and Ian began immediately to spurt out their own fantasies, Jason insisted, "just *you,* Don, not you guys."

Because of Jason's intensity in asking the question, I took it more seriously than the usual banter we engage in, and found myself in quiet reflection as I drove along while Ian and Tano rattled off boyish dreams of houses that sprouted money, the ability to transport in space, having a Lamborghini, and every possible PlayStation2 game.

The very first thing that came forth was "Health for our family this summer." When I said this, I realized its truth was about as solid as any I might imagine. We were about to embark on a two-week packing trip near the tree line of the Colorado Rockies. Tano had just contracted a bad cold, which typically developed into debilitating asthma. I desperately wanted him to get well fast, and for my wife and me to escape catching his infection. At that moment, I couldn't imagine anything else in the world I wanted more.

Moreover, it was not a futile utopian longing: its realization was something humanly possible, if not certain. Over the years we had learned how to deal with Tano's recurrent bouts of colds and asthma with regimens of medicine, allergy controls, and rest. If we were meticulous in applying what we knew, the probabilities were in our favor.

It took me a few more minutes of quiet reflection to come up with wish number two, while Tano and Ian kept interjecting their wild fantasies of being able to fly backwards like Neo in *The Matrix* or drive sports cars over cliffs like *XXX*'s Vin Diesel. "I would like to finish the manuscript I've been working on," I said, "and succeed in getting it published and widely read."

Like wish number one, this one felt like it bubbled up uncontrived from somewhere deep inside: I truly wanted this, felt I could accomplish this if I maintained my courage in the light of the obstacles that face any author, and considered it important to the life of my soul.

A third wish was slow in coming. Jason kept insisting that I finish while the other two boys fantasized away. I found myself entertaining life-long concerns about serious wounds in the larger world. As we approached the end of our drive, I said, "I wish that we would elect a president who would mobilize the people to create a better world for when you guys grow up."

Although the wish did come from an authentic longing for a more humane world beyond the immediacy of our private life, my articulation of it felt too mental, hackneyed, and ideological. I felt a desire to do what I could to see that my son and his generation would not have to face an adulthood in a Blade Runner or Soylent Green world, stripped of forests and rife with high-tech violence. But I know that no one man or woman can radically alter the world, especially a political man or woman. Though the outcomes of my first two wishes were not mathematically certain, they were humanly possible if I stayed alert and courageous in actually doing what I was capable of. Number three was like an un-earned solution to a complex drama, a *deus ex machina* who flies in from offstage to save the actors from their tragedies just in time for the show to end. Worse than that, it was the kind of ungrounded hope that can easily lead to disillusionment, as happened to my father when he approached the end of his life and saw the once-fresh world around him turning sour.

The few minutes in the car with those boys afforded me an opportunity to see beyond the familiar differences between the wild fantasies of the young and the world-weary scepticism of the old. My halting expressions against the backdrop of their cascade of dreams reflected my long life of determining what I really want in relation to what is humanly possible. In this work, I have tried to locate a more authentic formulation of my third wish, a family of hopes for our larger world, neither exclusively mundane nor too wildly utopian. Such hopes would have to have the sanity that takes account of the fact that we live in an increasingly diverse world—cultural, religious, dietary, and many other categories of specialness. They would also have to be buttressed by a resilience and courage needed to cope with the obvious crises that will confront these children in their lifetimes. Hopes that depend on gated communities populated only by a certain class of people with similar tastes in clothes and religion cannot withstand the pressures of this world in which we find ourselves.

2

The Mundane
and the Apocalyptic

I was born in Sacramento, and lived in California most of my life. I learned to swim in the Sacramento and the American, before the dams. I learned to drive on the levees up and downriver from Sacramento. Yet California has remained in some way impenetrable to me, a wearying enigma, as it has to many of us who are from there. We worry it, correct and revise it, try and fail to define our relationship to it and its relationship to the rest of the country.

—Joan Didion, *Where I Was From*[2]

MY WIFE BARBARA, MY SON TANO, AND I often camp, hike, and ski high up in the Sierra Nevada on the eastern rim of the Central Valley of California. From the Pacific Crest Trail at 11,000 feet you can look down from Donner Summit or the Mono Divide towards Auburn, Escalon, and Lodi and see the results of the decisions made over the past 150 years since the first incursions of immigrants from the Old Worlds and from the older states beyond the mountains. Those heights afford a high-altitude, exhilarating spectacle of unimaginably prolific natural gifts stretching out far beyond the rolling granite summits, the snowfields, and carpets of alpine flowers. And at the same time, you can see the depressing extent to which we have betrayed nature's generosity.

The primeval networks of marshes with their millions of migratory birds, the fish-rich deltas, and oak-garbed foothills—where there were once scattered thatched villages of Pomo and Modoc—are now laced with freeways to gated communities, quaint bed-and-breakfasts, and gambling palaces. The delta soils are weighed down under mountains of manure from industrial cattle-feeding lots, toxic pesticides from the corporate ranches, and industrial pollutants from the processing plants. Smog from the rapidly metastasizing automobile and truck populations creeps up towards the tree line, over which are strung the endless cables for ski lifts.

The present shape of the Central Valley is the result of a series of social experiments, where the human mind has revealed its genius as well as its serious deficiencies—the shapes of its unlimited capacities for imagination and creativity, as well as its hunger for fast wealth unchecked by virtue. When I was born at the end of the Great Depression, hope saturated the air all around us. You could see it glimmering on the snow-capped Sierras to the east, the Irish-green hills of the Pacific Range in the west, Mt. Lassen and Mt. Shasta in the north; and the vast empty skies to the south. You could smell its fragrances rising from the fields of crops planted in the riverbottom loam alongside the levees. You could hear its signals of a better future in the night whistles of the railroad engines that brought my great-grandmother and all my grandparents to the end of the line of the first transcontinental railroad, built by Mark Hopkins, Charles Crocker, Leland Stanford, and Collis Huntington, the "Big Four" who began accumulating their fortunes selling supplies to the gold-seekers in their dry goods and grocery stores in the neighborhood where my family settled.

My ancestors grew up in the straitened ecosystems of the Norwegian fjords and the Burrens of Ireland. Like most others who settled in California in the 1800s, they wanted to leave history and any criminal charges behind in the stinking slums and impoverished farms where many of them were reared. There was a freshness in that absence of connection with history—and, at the same time, tragic dangers. To them, the sheer vastness of the Sacramento Valley made it virtually impossible to imagine that one could build too many roads, put too much fertilizer and garbage in the soil, or have any noticeable effect on the limitless sky above us. There was so much of everything—fruit and vegetables, trout, ducks and pheasants, fertile topsoil, clean air. With so many crystalline rivers flowing everywhere, never more than ten miles apart, they could not foresee the water shortages that now threaten.

My mother, who was born in Sacramento in 1908, still reminisces about how safe the town felt before the intrusions of interstates and airports, sealed off from the violence and hardships of the Old Worlds by the Sierra Nevada and the Coast Range, cozily nestled within the confluence of the Sacramento and American Rivers, protected by levees on all sides. It had the ecology of ancient Baghdad or Paris, settlements on marshy crossroads surrounded by rivers and lush farmland, moderate climate, no bone-chilling ice-storms nor tornadoes, with the great earthquake faults a hundred miles to the west.

The hopes that thickened the moist Valley air even at that early period were different enough to generate conflicts among different branches of my family. One kind of hope was earthy; it sprung from close-to-home and grounded desires for an easier daily life than was available in the Old Worlds. Another kind was apocalyptic, fueled by visions of cataclysmic destruction of this world, to be replaced by a radically different world yet to be revealed, where justice and love prevail over human folly. A third was somewhere in between, a more sober hope for an eternal future in another world, but with an emphasis on our behavior in this world as the key required for entry.

My father's family fueled themselves on modest hopes, mundane in the old Latin sense of "earthy," focused on this life. They were plain people, scrupulously ethical but without much interest in the more unworldly ideals of formal religion. They came here from a Scandinavia whose arable land was too scarce to support a growing population. They wanted a more comfortable life in a less severe terrain, with less danger of famine, perhaps even a modest ascent into the middle classes with the pleasures and leisure afforded by that rise. Their dreams were not those of nation-builders or conversion-obsessed missionaries, but of ordinary folk whose lives are occupied with constructing an easier life for their families in a unique land filled with chances for a first automobile, an extra bedroom for the children, a more functional bathroom, a few days more vacation a year, and better cuts of meat on the table.

Born of a long line of Norwegian coffin-makers, my grandfather Jul Olaf Johnson emigrated from Oslo to Minnesota in the 1880s, when their name was changed to Johnson from an unknown name over which my family still argues, perhaps Jensen or Johansson. According to one of the meagre family stories about their Old World past, Jul talked about how his forebears had made a living during rough times in Norway by traveling to Germany to do woodwork on the Rhine castles. He had a quiet sense of irony about him, not easy, often arguing with my father, and bossing around his wife Matilda and daughters Gladys and Charlotte. He was my favorite relative because I had fun with him. He taught me to play pinochle and poker when I was only five years old, and gave me my first glass of beer. In the evenings and weekends, he would usually play pool or cards across the street at the M Street Café, a bar with floor-to-ceiling windows where you could look in and see everything going on. He always worked hard as a carpenter and was roofing a grain silo out by the river until two days before he died of liver cancer in his late sixties.

Jul met my grandmother Matilda Otilia Turnbloom at a local dance club for Scandinavian immigrants. It was the second time she had emigrated to Sacramento. The first was in 1880, when as a young teenager she sailed to Panama with her older brothers Andy and Charley from Göteborg, Sweden, took the train across the Isthmus, and a ship up the coast to San Francisco, then the steamer up the river. Not long after, she returned to Sweden and then back again to Sacramento for reasons we never knew, but I always assumed she must have been intensely unhappy to make such long and arduous journeys. Even in her later years when I knew her, I sensed in her a longing for the Old Country. Her best friend Thecla lived a few blocks away, and the two of them would while away the afternoons over coffee speaking Swedish as long as my grandfather was not around to forbid them on the reasoning that they were Americans and had to act like such.

Although, like all Swedes and Norwegians, they had been baptized as Lutherans, neither my father, his parents, nor his sisters ever went to church, even on Christmas and Easter. I never heard them speak of religion.

Grandpa Jul and my father passed on to me a sense that the tangible world is indeed changeable and that our hard work has the capacity to leave visible traces on that world. They built many of the original houses in the city, including their own, which still remain like new, solid, thickly insulated against the heat and cold, with hardwood floors and redwood shake roofs, expanded with second stories and upscaled with tiles and porticoes by the new upper middleclasses who have settled in the old city. Like the Taos Pueblo, their constructions were not fancy, but durable. My family has lived in the center of the old city since my great-grandmother Lucy settled there on T Street in 1870. (What is now known as "Old Town," a four-block stretch of shops and restaurants along the waterfront, was actually built in the 1970s and made to appear to be very old to draw tourists.) My mother was born a few blocks from where my father was born. Capitol Park was in the neighborhood, as was the grand old gothic Governor's Mansion eventually abandoned by Ronald and Nancy Reagan because, Mrs. Reagan said, it had too many bookshelves and not enough closets and wet bars. My dad and Grandpa Jul stored their house-building materials in a barn on the lot around the corner from their house on N Street where they would build our house in 1939.

I had a sense of location in the cosmos from growing up and seeing our marks throughout the expanding city, the many reflections in the everyday world that we were truly *here*. There are still traces left by my work as a teenager on survey crews laying out the terraces of Capitol Park, the gardens of California State College, the extensions of the city out beyond Land Park, and the network of freeways surrounding the city.

I wonder in my bleaker moments, however, if there is any real point to those material effects of our work. The houses are not remarkable, but are plain, simple dwellings that anyone with skill might have built. Unlike a few others of the same era whose more aesthetic designs and finer materials are recognizable in various parts of the city, they exhibit little flair or idiosyncratic quirks of imagination. My own marks are of no more significance than the piss of animals staking out their territories.

Despite such doubts, this feeling of efficacy provided a foundation for a sane hope in the future. Unlike the utopian dreams of religion and philosophy in which I became enmeshed as a young adult, the Johnson hopes seem closer to our basic capacities for doing things: a sense that we can improve our dwellings, help our neighbors when they are in need, maybe even make the larger neighborhood safer, improve our schools, make our food taste better and be more nourishing.

The only larger-than-life notions the Johnsons had was a romance about the American frontier—ideals of the cowboy and prospector, embodied in my two great-uncles Andy and Charley, Grandma Matilda's brothers, the John Waynes of our family, the kind of men who dared to penetrate the empty frontier, carving out substantial room for their children in the wide-open West. Uncle Andy built one of the last gold mines of that era along the American River near Folsom, where his house still stands on the only rise in town, deeded over to his three daughters. He was about as close as our family ever got to the legendary California fortunes. An early twentieth-century photograph of his gold mine hangs on my son's wall. He, my grandfather Jul, my young father, and ten other workers stand on the sluice float in front of the conveyor belt dredging up the gold-bearing river rocks, which were left in the piles you can still see today driving up Highway 50 towards Placerville. The men in their cocked fedoras, arms akimbo, have the proud and defiant look of pirates of the Mother Lode.

My aunts say that because Uncle Charley got a girl pregnant, he was packed off to the wastelands of southeastern Oregon where, funded by Andy's gold, he homesteaded a section of land for cattle-raising along Wildhorse Creek. Eventually a small town grew up along the road nearby which was named "Andrews" after Charley's benevolent brother. Every summer from when my dad was nine years old, Matilda and Jul put him on a bus for the two-day trip up across the Donner Pass into Reno, then directly north through Winnemuca where he spent the night in a hotel, then on to work for the summer at the ranch. I have a photo of him, Uncle Charley, and the cowpokes on their horses against the windbreaks with the herd ranging the grassy plains, their gazes looking out over a wide-open world.

My father always reminisced about those summers as if they were the happiest of his life: his long journey on the Greyhound, a night alone in a Winnemuca hotel, learning how to handle a horse and brand cattle, bunking down with the cowpokes. Throughout my boyhood, I often heard him talking of an odd fantasy that Charley would deed him the ranch when he died on the argument that Charley had only daughters. Such a peculiar line of reasoning must have been a residue inherited from an Old World mentality that only men could own land. The daughters, of course, eventually did inherit it, contributing to my father's dashed hopes. I imagine that his delusion was his way of clinging to an unclear dream of a wild and quiet place where he could ride the range far from an increasingly complex urban life, which required more education and skill than he was raised with. He always seemed restless, wanting something more out of life than he could find in our neighborhood. The restlessness eventually turned into a bitterness that soured his final years.

There are photographs of me as early as three years old sitting on a pony in Land Park wearing cowboy hat, chaps, and heavy leather belt with a holster holding my silver cap-gun with mother-of-pearl handle. One of my earliest memories is of the 1939 centennial celebration of the founding of Sacramento, when I was allowed to sit in the driver's seat of a real stagecoach sponsored by The Friend and Terry Lumber Company, where my father and Grandpa Jul bought materials for their house-building business. Dressed in cowboy gear, we rode in a parade from the lumber yard on the waterfront around Southside Park, where a mockup had been constructed of the original settlement, with its forges and stockades to keep out the Indians. I sat high on the stagecoach-driver's seat with a perfect view of everything. Even today, I recall the thrill I felt on that perch, sensing that I was an heir to the pioneering spirit of cowboys and miners. After sunset, fireworks shot high over the big fishpond, while my family ate hot dogs on the grass. By the time I reached third grade I had my own horse, hand-tooled saddle and boots, spurs, leather chaps, Stetson, and a pearl-button cowboy shirt. For my tenth birthday, my father bought me an 1890 Winchester double-barrel 20-gauge shotgun, and he began to take me hunting for pheasant, duck, quail, and dove.

Despite the humane sanity that marked the dense materiality of my father and his family, it also had a sluggishness close to chronic depression, as if their dreams were not vital enough to carry them through the challenges that they had to face. In witnessing their growing sense of despair as they grew older, I saw that worldly hopes alone are not enough to sustain a life. Unchecked by more spacious desires for whole-heartedness, compassion, creativity, and ecstasy, a sense of material efficacy alone has led to the virtual destruction of many of the natural gifts the Valley had to offer my family. Like the once-fertile triangle between the Tigris and Euphrates, this "New World Eden" is being turned into a wasteland by short-sighted greed and passive ignorance.

I inherited an other-worldly set of hopes from my mother's religiously devout side of the family. Her grandmother and my great-grandmother Lucy represented the most extreme form of that kind of hope. She and her daughters Rose—my grandmother who died as a young woman—and Ann were among the first passengers on the Union Pacific railroad, arriving in Sacramento in the 1870s from Roodhouse, a small town in Illinois. When I knew her, Lucy was in her late eighties and had survived three husbands. She wore long old-fashioned dresses, the kind you see in movies about the old West, which she sewed herself. I loved staying at her house overnight when I was a toddler, cozily buried in a thick featherbed by a wood stove. She had chickens in the backyard and a vegetable garden.

Although she outwardly lived a pedestrian life like my father's parents, she had a secret life apart from ours, which I imagined must have been fervently spiritual. She regularly attended the local Baptist church, frowned upon both by my father's and mother's sides of the family for its immodest styles of worship. To my mother's consternation, as Lucy approached ninety she converted to the Jehovah's Witnesses, an even more religiously immodest sect. I wondered whether this plain, seemingly austere woman actually engaged in the wild hollerings and rollings of their ecstatic church worship. A glossy, brightly colored calendar hung on her wall with a large picture of a gigantic raging Jehovah looming over hordes of devils and angels, Jesus meekly looking up at Him and pleading for the miserable sheep-like sinners hiding behind his cloak. I remember being confused by its depiction of our Pope Pius XII burning in the depths of Hell with the title of "Antichrist" in bold letters underneath. My mother attributed Lucy's beliefs to senility, even though she seemed at least as bright and alert as anyone else in our family. In her early nineties, Lucy dropped dead on a downtown corner across from the Catholic cathedral, our parish church, on a hundred-degree summer afternoon as she was giving out *The Watchtower,* urging its readers to prepare for the end of the world in a divine holocaust preceded by the Rapture which, according to the billboard at our street corner, was scheduled to arrive at the beginning of the following October.

I attribute to Lucy the origins of my life-long fascination with apocalyptic thinkers like the fraticelli of St. Francis, Giambattista Vico, William Blake, Norman O. Brown, Karl Marx, and Wilhelm Reich—people who theorize about sudden volcanic transformations of this sick and fragmented world into a more pleasing and just Utopia, from which the wicked or the psychologically repressed will be cast into eternal darkness. As she approaches one hundred years old, my mother show signs of inheriting some of that apocalyptic vision, despite her more modest religious devotion. She often refers to Lucy when conversations turn to the relentless news accounts of wars, ecological disasters, economic collapse, epidemics and famine, and the crass immorality of the wealthy and powerful. Perhaps, she says, Lucy was right: Armaggedon is at hand.

I was raised by my mother as a Roman Catholic somewhere in between the mundane metaphysics of my father's family and Lucy's apocalypticism. She and my Irish-born grandfather Joe Hanlon were scrupulously observant of that religion's arcane rules governing ritual obligations, food, sex, and other matters. But they were very quiet about it. While Catholic beliefs did have a magical cast, they always were situated within a conventional social world of good manners and extreme rationality. I learned only in catechism class about the more exotic beliefs that Three Divine Persons, along with angels, devils, and saints, were always hovering about us in cosmic battle over our immortal souls destined, depending on the battles' outcomes, to end up in an eternity of bliss or excruciating pain. Nuns and our parish priest were the first to inspire me with notions of re-making the world to eliminate violence, poverty, and hunger in the spirit of Jesus and the Prophets. I grew up singing in the language of old Rome, with strong traces of that old empire in its costumes and rituals, its demands for studying classical literature, and its mission to conquer the world for Jesus.

Unlike the vigorous Johnsons, my mother's family seemed cowed by the suffering that brought them to a place where few shared their beliefs. They sat passively on the sidelines of the vital new California life all around us, like a sleeper cell planning for a future life, infinitely more joyous than this tragic one.

Joe Hanlon, the last of eight children, had been born towards the end of the nineteenth-century potato famine to an impoverished farming family in the tiny village of Kilbeggan, midway on the road between Gallway and Dublin. His mother died giving him birth. His father made two trips across the Atlantic and the Continent to gather his children to Sacramento, where his own siblings had already settled. Joe was brought there on the second trip when he was only two years old. I see him in photographs of Christian Brothers High School, where he graduated in 1896. He and his classmates sit in classic wooden desks, elegantly erect in high starched white collars, ties, vests, and suits. The Irish brothers hover gloomily behind them. I have his graduation portrait, taken when he must have been about eighteen. He looks like a quiet dandy in his stiff white collar, ascot tie, hair neatly parted down the middle, a pretty face, without expression, looking sadly bereft.

Like Jul and Matilda, Joe met Rose Pryor at a dance club, this one a weekly event at the Senator Hotel, across from the State Capitol, down the block from his men's clothing store, where he worked most of his life. My mother says they loved to waltz together, and did so regularly. They married and gave birth to my mother. I have a photo of them walking through Capitol Park. It is the only image I have of him—either in picture or memory—in which he appears happy, even jaunty. They are dressed to the nines, my grandmother Rose in a long full swirling skirt, fluffy white blouse, an enormous broad-brimmed hat with ostrich feathers, smiling at the camera, in love. When my mother was approaching her thirteenth birthday, Rose fell into a long illness whose nature my mother never knew until she died of breast cancer when the bells of the Cathedral sounded the turn of the 1921 new year.

By the time I was born, Joe had settled into a chronic depression. Despite the fact that I was born in his house and spent most of my life until college living with him, or with him living in our new house, I know virtually nothing about his interior life. He said and did very little: walked to work across Capitol Park every day to his store, came home, ate dinner with us, then sat reading the paper or listening to the news and sports events on the radio. On a few occasions he went out on Sunday afternoons with a "lady" whom he had met through some single person's network. He was a baseball fan and often walked over to the stadium on Broadway to see the Sacramento Solons.

Everything about him was well crafted. In his woodshop out in back of our house, he made for me intricate and realistic hand-tooled models of Roman catapults and medieval cross-bows, which were the envy of all the boys in our neighborhood because they functioned as actual weapons, hurtling stones and arrows for long distances. He wrote only with quill pen in Gothic script with India ink: envelopes to creditors, Christmas cards, and occasional notes to me when I was away at college. It's as if he were carrying on the two-thousand-year-old tradition of monks spending their lives in remote scriptoria, mindlessly yet artfully copying the Bible and the pagan classics to preserve a wisdom whose actual content was unknown to most of them. I never saw him write just a simple plain word with a pencil in cursive, just as I never saw him out of formal business attire. Unlike Grandpa Jul—who was a manual laborer, swarthy, lean, and muscular, always in work clothes—Joe was always in a suit, vest, collared shirt with cufflinks, and tie, even when he was in the house living with us, or working in the backyard. Although he would doff his coat around the house or while working in the backyard, I don't remember ever seeing him without his vest or without a long-sleeve dress shirt even in the intense heat of Sacramento summers.

When my parents went out at night on the weekends, the house felt so lonely with only the two of us there in silence. I grew up taking Joe's minimal activity as normal, but now I think of it as a tableau of nearly pathological depression. I have a memory of my mother and father talking quietly one night, thinking I couldn't hear them, about my mother's having found a pistol in Joe's drawer and worrying that he was thinking of suicide. When I try to find my way into his head, I imagine what it would be like to lose one's mother at birth, be brought across the ocean and the continent as a two-year-old, raised by older siblings in a strange land, then falling in love only to lose a beloved after a short life with her. Though my mother's life has been very different—her marriage long and happy, her needs well cared for—she also fell into a similar depression. With her mother dying just as she was entering puberty, she seemed unable ever to grieve and leave behind that sad memory. Like her father, part of her seemed to have died long before I was born.

Fending off their bleak histories with religious faith, Grandpa Joe and my mother passed on to me their Roman Catholic hopes for a glorified humanity, the City of God whose citizens are kinder and more generous, and all of whom agree on the meaning of life. Even though my father's parents seemed more humane, earthy, and with a taste for ordinary pleasures, I craved the excitement of Roman Catholic and Evangelical stories of Satan battling the archangels, Jesus healing the sick and rising from the dead, and saints appearing in dreams. Before television, PlayStation, and CGI, those exotic and often bloody stories dragged me out of the hypnotic Delta miasmas.

Within that gnarled skein of religious beliefs, I have had to search for clues on how to reconcile three seemingly incompatible tendencies: the mundane devotion to carrying on a successful life in this world without falling into despair or greed; the development of humane virtues like courage, affection, and patience, without falling into a puritan moralism; and the ability to enjoy the most ecstatic dimensions of human experience without becoming a fanatic.

3

Speed Limits

//

I believed in movement. That was the theme of California. People were coming to California to begin life anew; I believed in the necessity of abandoning Sacramento, if I were ever to amount to anything. But it was the same impulse. I assumed there would be room enough on the freeway for my ambition.

—RICHARD RODRIGUEZ, *Brown*[3]

RICHARD, TEN YEARS YOUNGER THAN I, grew up a few blocks away from our house out towards Sacred Heart Church and, like myself, graduated from Christian Brothers High School. I find in his memoirs features of the world I knew: in this passage, movement. It was everywhere—houses being torn down to make way for new and larger ones, tracts of land being leveled for new developments, one job being changed for another, people always on the move and ideally up. And myself, too, I grew up with a desire deep in my bones to get out, get up, get anywhere but where I was, and fast. The speed, while invigorating for the blood and brain, would also exacerbate the tendency to leap to conclusions, making short-sighted decisions both personally and socially.

As long as I can remember I have been in cars in the Valley, driven or driving: the earliest times in the late 1930s when I was four. On Sunday afternoons my father would borrow his father Jul's gray Ford roadster and I would ride in the open bumper seat over to the duck pond at William Land Park. One day I fell in the pond thinking I could walk on top of the lily pads. My father laughed at me, calling me stupid as he often did, and I felt humiliated, sowing the seeds of a rage that would brew so long that it would eventually eat away at our relationship. Later in the day all of the family might drive way out Freeport Boulevard to the inn whose roof extended over the road. My father and Grandpa Jul would swallow jalapeño peppers until the sweat ran down their brows and their eyes watered, and wash it down with drafts of Buffalo Beer. On hot summer evenings he, my mother, and I would get into his Ford pickup and drive out towards Elk Grove or down the river towards Ryde, stopping for an ice cream at Borden's dairy on the way back home.

In that pre-freeway era of two- and three-lane highways, we were always on the road, out into the country to picnic on the sloughs, up to ski and sled the slopes of the Sierras before there were resorts, on to Lake Tahoe to swim, the Feather River fishing, Colusa to shoot ducks, Jackson for homemade ravioli, Stockton for the best tamales from the Pioneer Tamale Factory. Although the abstract geographical distance from Redding to Bakersfield is about the same as from Boston to Washington, DC, or from Paris to Rome, the experiential distance was much shorter. A new attitude towards driving was being born here. To drive from Boston to Washington or Paris to Rome was not an everyday occurrence to be taken lightly without serious forethought. But automobiles were so natural to the life of the Valley that adults would take on trips of that distance as if they were perfectly ordinary. The new towns were already being shaped to accommodate fast-driving automobiles. While Los Angeles was still a modest city with no freeways and ample public transportation, the Valley was gearing up for the vehicles that would eventually flood in from Detroit, Bremen, and Tokyo. The designers of the new farming towns sprouting around the Valley had such an unfettered notion of available space that they laid out the streets wider than any of their ancestors in the Old Worlds had ever imagined. Even though the little sidestreets in small towns like Williams, Manteca, or Firebaugh were officially two-lane, they were big enough for four, and the main streets were as wide as the freeways eventually would be.

Much of our family time together was in automobiles. Even short trips on a map seemed to take forever. Air conditioning had not yet been invented. Car heaters spurted forth only the mildest warmth, and the engines of that era often broke down. Because highways were constantly under construction, traffic was always delayed. The most lasting memories of those difficulties are of my father's impatience about wasting any time stopping to let my mother or me go to the bathroom. I often had to hold my pee for what seemed like hours waiting to get to our destination. To this day, I feel nervous getting into a car for a long drive. Even though I know mentally that I can stop whenever I want, my body seems never to have freed itself from those earlier memories. My father's impatience was always clouding our trips. One summer, we were preparing to leave for a vacation at Santa Cruz, which was a long day's drive away on narrow two-lane roads through Stockton and Livermore to San Jose and over the Santa Cruz mountains. My father got so upset with my mother for taking a long time to pack our bags that he stormed out of the house and didn't come back by the time we were ready to go. A friend of my parents, whose family was already down there, had planned to go with us. To my mother's humiliation, he ended up driving us down without my father. When my father finally appeared at our cabin late that night in his pickup, I pretended to be asleep while I listened to muffled arguments between him and my mother. As a boy, I felt utterly helpless in the face of my father's rage; I couldn't imagine changing anything in our situation. Unlike the efficacy I learned to feel as an apprentice contractor, I developed a sense of impotence about human conflict.

✧

Although it was gearing up in the 1930s, the driving culture took off full speed with the end of gasoline rationing after World War II. My father became a partner in a heavy construction company that laid gas and water lines throughout the West. Every day, he drove to job sites throughout the Valley and into Nevada. During elementary school vacations, I often went with him in his Dodge pickup with its hard seats. The trips seemed interminable in the hot cab filled with smoke from my father's cigarettes, with me spending hours waiting while he inspected various stages of the pipelines, snaking down from the high Sierra lakes through Sonora, over Carson Pass into Virginia City, down from the Hetch Hetchy through Manteca, over the Coachella Pass into Santa Barbara.

The proliferation of the water projects, whose sources were the hundreds of glacial lakes, would lead to the seediest deals in California politics as the post-war population burgeoned and Valley agribusiness became the largest in the world. My childhood playmate Joan Didion would grow up to write about the shadowy sides of those politics, taking up the heritage of her grandfather, a hydraulics engineer, who was the first to map those sources and publish a book about them.

The first summer after the War, my father won a bid for a job in the small town of Hawthorne on Walker Lake in Nevada, where there is still an army ammunition dump and rocket-launching station. It seemed to take forever to drive there along Highway 50 over Echo Summit, cutting off south of Lake Tahoe over to Gardnerville and down through Fallon to Hawthorne, nearly a full day's drive. The truck often broke down. I spent a few weeks there with him in a little motel, working during the day as a water-boy. The pipeline began near a watertower. With each day, the crew moved further and further from the tower, which meant that my walks through the hot desert sun to refill the water jugs got progressively longer, until I would arrive at the tower hot and exhausted, gaze at the men and equipment far in the distance, and feel that I would never make it back. I began to wonder if this was the life I faced as a man—hard, bleak work whose only point was the paycheck and the pleasures it would afford. At night, I ate in a local saloon with my father and his crew, feeling like I was being inducted into the secret society of men, thick Nevada beefsteak and potatoes followed by ice cream and apple pie. I had my first taste of serious gambling, and came back home with twenty dollars more than I started with.

Another job my father gave me that summer was to document the educational background of his crew to meet government regulations. I remember being startled that virtually no one had schooling beyond third or fourth grade. By then I had come to associate intelligence with the level of schooling one had completed. But the men on the crew seemed to me as thoughtful as many of my parents' friends back in Sacramento who had completed at least twelve grades. Everyone called these men Oakies and Arkies. They were the second wave of refugees from the Dust Bowl, the first of which occurred in the 1930s and was described by John Steinbeck in *The Grapes of Wrath*. Many were post-war immigrants from Yugoslavia and Poland who had worked the oilfields in Arkansas, Texas, and Oklahoma, and then followed the pipelines westward. I remember the first time I went out to visit one of the workers' homes when I was around ten years old. My father and I crossed the American River into an unfamiliar neighborhood nestled in the floodplain under the levees. It was not so much a neighborhood as a camp—tiny clapboard houses, converted trailers, and boxes. We were going to see my father's foreman, his highest-paid employee. I have such a clear memory of my bewilderment on entering a tiny two-room house with two parents and nine children living in it, a first moment of awakening to the poverty in which much of the world lives invisible.

I had a brush with catskinning on that trip to Hawthorne. "Cat" refers to the various kinds of heavy earth-moving equipment produced by John Deere Caterpillar, which are "skinned" by manipulating their complex levers and control buttons. Heavy machinery was for me in the same class as Flash Gordon's rocket ships and the Batmobile—signs of adult male power, tools for blasting out of the impotence of childhood. My dad, anxious to initiate me into a key work of his trade, set me on a relatively small "blade," a tractor with a heavy wide steel blade in front used to push piles of dirt back into the ditches and smooth them over. The blade, in that now-outdated design, was suspended by a steel cable that was pullied overhead, anchored to a winch in the rear, played out by a complex set of gears. My dad first showed me how to move the tractor about, then the blade. I felt on top of the world manipulating this heavy monster, pushing heaps of dirt. He finally felt confident enough to let me do a little of the backfilling myself. I was moving happily along when suddenly my hand slipped on the control of the gears that ensured a smooth lowering of the blade. The blade dropped, snapping the overhead cable. My father was furious with me, red in the face, fuming. I felt humiliated in front of the snickering work crew. I didn't want to skin it again, nor did I ever. I had failed in this first test of mastering big machines, which along with sports and hunting marked progress on the way to manhood.

The next summer it was different. For the first time in my life, in school or out, I met a man who could actually help me succeed at a man's task. Then twelve years old, I was again spending a good part of vacation with my father, whose construction company was putting in water and sewer lines for Escalon, a small farming town on the road from Stockton to Yosemite. He apprenticed me to

Joe Hug, a gruff sixty-five-year old who drove a large water truck needed to force-pump water into loosely back-filled ditches to compact their surface level so as not to disrupt the roads and driveways under which the pipelines traveled. I manned the four-inch hose, pushing it deep into the soft backfill, while he inched along in the cab. Although he didn't talk much, I could tell by his friendly demeanor that he was growing to like me. He was a Polish immigrant with only a third-grade education, small, bent-over, arthritic, eyes failing. He had been the getaway driver for Al Capone in Chicago, and for reasons I never knew, had moved to California and gotten a job as a driver for my father. Inching slowly down the ditch lines in the searing hot afternoons, he enjoyed regaling me with stories of the many bank robberies and shootouts he claimed to have been involved in. Capone died that summer, and Joe took off work for a couple of days to go back to Chicago for the funeral.

It was a less crowded and speedy time in the Valley, when there were still many country roads that saw few cars. During those long hot days together driving at a snail's pace along the ditches, then going back through town to reload the water-tank, Joe began letting me drive the truck. He had patience with my raw youth, unlike my father and a few other adults who thought I should be able to pick up a basketball or get on a cat and learn how to do it right away, and if I didn't I was just dumb. Unlike my grade-school teachers and religion teachers who thought of children as empty vessels to be filled with information, Joe taught by getting me to pay attention to the feel of the vehicle: sensations of the clutch engaging and disengaging to different foot pressures and speeds, sounds of the gears as they went higher or lower and the engine as it speeded up or slowed down, the pull and give of the steering wheel, the resistances of the brake. He taught me how important it was to relax behind the wheel so I could more easily pay attention to all these sensations as well as watch the road ahead and behind and sideways.

I guessed that Joe's skill developed through negotiating fast get-aways. It would be impossible to drive away from a bank in down-town Chicago with the cops in hot pursuit if he were relying on the slow, clunky, rational mind for calculating how to negotiate all the necessary moves. Like an expert martial artist fending off the blow of a sword, or an airplane pilot negotiating a wind-shear, he was successful because he had developed the capacity to sense and process bewildering complexes of data in an instant.

After that summer of driving the hulky water truck slowly down the quiet roads of Escalon, learning to brake, shift, accelerate, come to a full stop and start up again, I continued to drive regularly with my father in his pickup on back roads in the Valley. By the time I reached legal age and took formal driving lessons, all that was left to learn was parallel parking and how to negotiate high-speed driv-ing on busy highways—relatively easy tasks given the solid feel I had by now acquired for the workings of any vehicle.

I recognized the importance of Joe's teaching style by contrast to teachers of the other skills I was trying to learn at that time when I was just entering puberty: penmanship (in that age of leaky fountain pens), golf, baseball, basketball, horseback riding, ballroom danc-ing. Elementary school teachers complained that I might have to be held back because I couldn't get my cursive letters to fit within the Parker Penmanship grids. Despite hours of instruction, I stopped riding the horse my father gave me for my ninth birthday because I never learned to develop a feel for the animal and it kept running away with me. I felt particularly shameful about playing baseball and basketball. All the boys did it, and my father desperately worked to teach me how. When he paid for uniforms for our school teams, the coaches gave me what I felt were unearned positions on the team, typically out in right field. But even so, my mind spun so widely at the plate that I could rarely concentrate my sensations on the bat handle and the trajectory of the ball. When I was in the outfield and saw

a ball arcing high in the air towards me, I got so confused I would
rarely be able to locate myself where I might catch it. The basketball
felt so huge and unwieldy in my hands, I could never manipulate it
with any skill. I finally quit all the teams I joined. Nor did I do much
better in academic courses, where I had a hard time mastering grammar, history, and geography. Against that backdrop of shame at my
failures to learn, Joe Hug stood out as the first of only a handful of
teachers who actually showed me how to go about developing a particular skill by teaching me to develop a feel for things, trusting that I
could figure out how to maneuver if I learned to pay more attention
to what was happening than to what people were thinking of me.

He embodied an unfamiliar kind of savvy, which I now associate with hopes resilient enough to weather the inevitable defeats of
daily life. The tough fibers that sustain such hopes are not the fine
lines on spare Cartesian grids of rationality; they are woven into the
dark textures of the unconscious. One finds them not by thought
alone, but by developing a full range of sensibilities to what draws
us forward, and to what enlivens us in the midst of the pains that
keep trying to defeat us.

✧

Vehicle speeds in the Valley have risen steadily since I was a
child. Now, if you keep to the 65-mph limit on the interstates or
the old Highway 99 you will feel like a laggard, everyone veering
around you, turning on their high beams right up on your bumper, like a European revving his Mercedes down the autobahn.
Everyone is in a desperate hurry to get somewhere else; there is no
reason to linger on these barren asphalt deserts, devoid of pleasure.
Movement, as Richard Rodriguez acutely observes, is indeed the
theme of California.

I have spent most of my adult professional life within a community of teachers and therapists specializing in bodily practices—sensory

awareness, breathing exercises, touch, movement awareness. A shared assumption of this large international community is that chronic speed condemns one to mechanical behavior, restricting one's ability to imagine fresh, effective solutions to the ongoing problems of life.

One innovator who was particularly concerned about the deleterious effects of speed on creative thinking was the late F. Matthias Alexander, a Tasmanian vaudeville actor who eventually moved to London, then to New York at the turn of the twentieth century where he developed the Alexander Technique, now widely used by musicians and artists. It is an approach to self-knowledge based on a careful and meditative reflection on the most basic activities of life, ranging from commonplace activities of standing, sitting, walking, and lying down to the specialized activities of one's work and play—lifting boxes, swinging a hammer, keyboarding, sculling, writing essays, imagining a more humane future. A fundamental strategy is what Alexander called "inhibition," which consists of the teacher's using words or hands to interrupt in mid-course the habitual completion of a particular activity so that the person has a fleeting moment to make the next step in a new way. Alexander thought of inhibition as more than a personal therapeutic tool, having implications for the way we make plans for the social world. In 1946, for example, reflecting on Hiroshima and Nagasaki, he wrote an essay on the implications of the atomic bomb:

> Obsolete indeed as were many of our ideas, conceptions, and beliefs, and so on before the advent of the present crisis, the past few years have completely altered the foundations of our previous ways of life, and it has become a matter of prime necessity to re-examine the pedigree of all such ideas, conceptions, and beliefs with which our overt activities are associated. To succeed in this, and to set about making the necessary changes to this end, we shall be forced to come to a FULL STOP. ... [Man]

has gradually been losing a reliable standard of control of reaction, and the ability to take the long view, in his efforts to improve his conditions when he is faced with the need for changing habits of thought and action. This should not surprise anyone who remembers that in most fields of activity man's craze is for speed and for the short view, because he has become possessed by the non-stop attitude and outlook ...[4]

Half a century later, speed has increased beyond what Alexander might ever have imagined. The requirements for profound and nuanced communal thought about our new creations become more demanding each day, and yet our actual thinking remains mired in old habits.

What Alexander called inhibition was an essential component of life in traditional cultures. Days were punctuated with ritual prayers from sunrise to sleep, reminding people of their gifts, their foibles, and their life purposes. During the sacred holidays, everything shut down for the long rituals and the communal feasts where people had the opportunity to take stock of their lives: the High Holy Days, Lent and Holy Week, Ramadan, the long Asian New Year festivals, ritual marriages and funerals, grace before and after meals. In Europe, there have been the hours-long siestas, the "bridges" over the weekends from the holidays that fall mid-week, the month of August, and often July, when all businesses close down except for those designed for tourists.

Long before I knew of Alexander, I chanced upon the life-changing potential of inhibition. In preparation for our graduation from the Jesuit University of Santa Clara in 1955, our senior class went to El Retiro in the Los Altos hills for a three-day silent retreat. I assumed it would be three days with my friends in a bucolic setting with good food and plenty of rest. Instead, I was visited by an apocalyptic disruption of my life's trajectory. Extended silence forced me up against the queasy nature of my mind. Left for long hours without occupation, my thoughts felt out of control, untutored and rude, like the annoying sounds of people behind us in the theater during a slow quiet film who continually whisper to each other about their impressions, making it difficult for us to remain absorbed by the screen. I had been jabbering for twenty-one years without ever stopping to ask myself what I really wanted from life. When the jabber stopped, it was utterly clear that I didn't want what I had geared my life for: a high-paying job in the corporate world, a glamorous wife, a family, and a sprawling ranch-style home in the Los Altos hills. In less than a year, I gave up the family dreams and entered the Jesuits, where I remained in a monastic setting for over a decade.

During my Jesuit studies, I encountered a little book that deepened my growing sense of the importance of inhibition in the development of wisdom. *The Silence of Saint Thomas,* by the German scholar Josef Pieper, was an essay on a little noticed event in the life of Thomas Aquinas, the thirteenth-century philosopher and theologian whose volumes were the model of reason for Catholic thinkers. During his fifty-second year, after finishing saying his daily mass, he turned to his server and scribe and said: "Compared to what I have experienced in today's mass, everything I have written is as straw." From that day until his death two years later, he didn't write a single word, leaving unfinished his monumental *Summa Theologiae.* Because he had been sainted and enshrined as the authority on the reasonableness of Catholic dogma—its ethical standards, theories of divine creation, the notions of the sacraments, and countless other theoretical underpinnings of the Church—no one before Pieper had taken this event seriously, brushing it off as a mystic's exaggeration or as a sign of the onset of senility. Challenging such dismissiveness, Pieper argued that Aquinas clearly demonstrated his seriousness by refusing to continue his life's work, particularly by leaving his *magnum opus* unfinished.

His analysis made perfect sense to me. A hot-blooded Tuscan adolescent joins the celibate religious order of Dominicans and feverishly channels all his fervor into making sense of these strange religious beliefs and his renunciation of what he admitted were overwhelming sexual desires, developing arcane, tortuous, hand-written texts about the most unearthly topics imaginable. In the midst of his daily mass, he stops. He finds himself between two worlds: one, a blissful divine realm offering pleasure beyond comprehension; and the other, a palpable world of suffering all about him—unceasing feudal wars and bloody crusades, ravages of the plagues, the hypocrisy of the Popes and bishops. Of what point are his delicate streams of Latin sentences in the face of these immense tides of the real? A stunned silence in the face of this situation makes perfect sense.

The notion of the scholar originated in the Greek word for leisure, *scholé,* at a time when Plato, Aristotle, and their followers realized that a new kind of community was being made possible by the freedom from an exclusive concern with physical survival. In this new community, at least a few had increasing time for conversing and thinking about less survival-oriented topics such as happiness, justice, and truth. As a few Greeks began to engage in leisure conversation after their daily naked exercises, they conceived of a community not structured around a single political figure or religious authority. At the same time, they became aware that the success of such a community placed new demands on thoughtfulness. If the community stopped relying on ready-to-wear thoughts articulated for centuries by shamans, priests, and kings, it had to find ways of weaving new ideas whole cloth: how to design a constitution and a moral code, educate young citizens, negotiate conflicts among people of radically different beliefs. In their view, such thinking required a good deal of leisure, quiet contemplation, and unpressured conversation with one's friends. The ideal of "leisure-ship" gave rise to Plato's Academy and Aristotle's Lyceum, the origins of the modern universities, driven by the vision of relying on quiet thought itself in conversation with other thoughtful people to imagine solutions to big questions and try them out.

Until the past century, such leisurely reflection was accessible only to an elite. In recent decades, however, the rise of a global middle class has given enormous populations the opportunity for hours, weeks, even months off work. In addition, there is the rapidly increasing population of elderly people who are healthy and alert for many years after they retire. Leisure has become one of the major industries in virtually every country in the world, even the most economically deprived. This new treasure-house of free time is rarely used as an opportunity for engaging in the kinds of educational and transformative activities that would increase our communal wisdom. Even those who claim the name of scholars are increasingly caught up in the marketplace, busily struggling to meet the demands of university productivity and cost-of-living increases.

My hope has been that as we have more time and quiet to think, we might imagine more effective ways of shaping a humane world. And yet, I often feel it is too late, that we have accelerated beyond our capacities to slow down. But in the spirit of Joe Hug, I keep trying for a better feel for the exact right moment and pressure to put on the brakes.

4

Slow Pleasures

I T IS HOPELESS TO IMAGINE THAT THE WORLD'S SPEED might be reduced by didactic exhortation or purely abstract thought. But
perhaps something might happen through pleasure, which slows
us down in enjoyment, giving us enough time to notice more details
about the people and world around us so that we might come up
with something new in our responses. F. M. Alexander's method has
been widely successful in inhibiting the speedy onrush of mechanical behavior because it does not rely on moral principles or rational
argument. Instead, it is designed to catch a person's attention by
attractive words and pleasurable touch. I still have vivid memories
of the luscious sensations I enjoyed during my first experience of
the technique more than three decades ago. During the course of a
standard session designed to engender fresh patterns of sitting and
standing by disrupting familiar habits, the teacher put her hand
very gently on my back as I moved up from a chair to standing, and
sat back down. The feeling of her hand gently shaping itself to the
nuanced contours of my back was so pleasurable that my incessant
interior gossip and automatic physical habits stopped in midflight.
The interior quiet of those moments of pleasurable contact gave
rise to new ways of getting up and sitting down.

"Slow Food" is an international movement created in 1986 by the
Italian Carlo Patrini, which now includes hundreds of thousands of
small farmers, food artisans, and chefs. Their mission is to rescue
countless old species of fruits, vegetables, cheeses, wines, and live-
stock, which are endangered by global corporations because they

are labor-intensive, take too long to cultivate, and do not ship well over long distances. These artisans and farmers recognize that their only hope for success in resisting the seemingly inexorable march towards the mass industrialization of food production lies not in moral righteousness but in appealing to people's enjoyment of the delights of taste and the vibrant health brought about by foods rich in vitamins, minerals, and enzymes in contrast to the impoverished products of the vast agribusinesses. Their motto is: "A firm defense of quiet material pleasure is the only way to oppose the universal folly of Fast Life."

These sane attitudes can seem wildly utopian in a culture like ours that views pleasure, at its best, as a trivial pursuit; worse, as an inducement to sin.

I have a friend in St. Petersburg, Russia, a microbiologist and granddaughter of two of the original revolutionaries. During a visit shortly before the demise of the Soviet Union, we spoke for hours about the history of their family. Her grandfather had been executed by Stalin, her grandmother sent to a Gulag where she died, and she herself had been in constant danger of imprisonment because of her activities in publishing underground Samizdat literature. I asked her what she thought had gone wrong with the revolutionaries that they ended up with this tragic collapse. She paused and made the surprising reply that they had no use for ordinary pleasures. Though strange at first glance, it made sense to me. She identified what had seemed to me to be a unique fact about the old Soviet Union and its Iron Curtain countries that made them different from other cultures I have known. On the streets there was no place for a quiet conversation over a cup of coffee. Restaurants were few and formal. There was little street food. Even in the countryside, you could not find a simple bakery, fruit stand, or café. You never heard music playing. Poets, actors, and other artists I met there confirmed that there had been an easy alliance between the old Orthodox ascetics who condemned the ordinary pleasures of life, and the Communists who succeeded them in power.

Nazism, Soviet Communism, and the various ascetic terrorist movements throughout the world, from Belfast to Ayacucho to Kabul, are but extreme examples of societies shaped by men who are so obsessed by abstractions about a perfect society, earthly or heavenly, that they cannot sense the agony in small children, women, and the very old. Against that violently moralistic backdrop, it is easier to appreciate the rationale behind a growing number of voices—Wilhelm Reich, Herbert Marcuse, Norman O. Brown, Michel Foucault, Susan Griffin, Susan Bordo, and others—who have argued that the cultivation of the body and its pleasures is a crucial and often neglected factor in social change.

It would seem odd to compare those devastated societies with our hedonistic culture, and yet, on closer inspection, the easy availability of every imaginable pleasure masks a deeper asceticism, which is linked both with speed and greed.

✧

By the time I was born in 1934, my parents were just climbing out of poverty. We were living crowded into my maternal grandfather Joe Hanlon's house. My father was weathering out the Depression, working on the line at Del Monte cannery until people once again had enough money to contract house-builders.

Despite the hard work my father and grandfather did to pull us out of immigrant poverty into a more comfortable life, working at their jobs sometimes as much as seven days a week, our lives never seemed to be as rushed as they are now. As the California boom began to take off after the War, they often complained that many of their friends had become so occupied with making money that they had no time to enjoy it. On Sacramento's many warm evenings, we would gather on Jul and Matilda's front porch, the adults sitting quietly in their chairs watching life on 19th Street, while my neighbor friends and I played in the alley. We spent much of our lives in my parents' long, narrow backyard where my father first began barbecuing on a tiny metal grill set on the ground. The portable gave way to a small brick barbecue, which my father expanded over the years into a brick and tile complex that was bigger than our kitchen. It had a sink, two ovens, a large adjustable grill and spit, chimney reaching higher than our grape-stake fence, and tiled patio with a dining table large enough to seat a dozen people. Whenever my father was home from his work on the road, he cooked dinner out there—pork ribs, whole racks of lamb, filet mignon, hamburgers, and sausages. Often he would barbecue breakfast in individual pans designed for two eggs, with grilled Canadian bacon.

In the years before the War, my father was a Nimrod like his forebears in Scandinavia. One of the four closets in our small house was stocked with his guns and fishing gear. On weekends, he would rise well before dawn and drive out to the marshes along the Sacramento River up towards Gridley and Colusa where, depending on the season, he would hunt duck, pheasant, dove, or quail. When he had more time, he would go out to Salt Point on the coast where he dove for abalone, plentiful then, now virtually extinct. On summer holidays, he would trek into the Sierras, sometimes on pack horses, to fish for trout. When he brought home the catch, the immaculate counters and floors of my mother's kitchen became a bloody workroom for the gutting and scaling of fish and game, and the pounding of the abalone with a large wooden mallet to render its legendary butter-like tenderness.

The balance between thoughtful and frivolous hunters shifted dramatically during the course of my growing up. After the War the wilds became increasingly crowded by leisurely hunters and fishermen, who were there more for a good time than for skillful engagement with prey sought as food. My father stopped hunting deer, complaining of the dangers arising from the mountains being so crowded with inexperienced and often tipsy men just having fun shooting. There were frequent mentions of the leisure classes moving up into the hunting grounds. Film stars like Bob Hope and Bing Crosby and wealthy industrialists were beginning to visit the upscale duck club in the rice paddies neighboring the fields where my father and his friends built a plain cabin on stilts in the wetlands of Butte Creek just north of the Sutter Buttes.

I grew up on a cuisine whose qualities I thought, in later life, had existed only in my imagination because I no longer found the tastes I associated with childhood. The Sacramento Valley was a garden of sensual delights. Like Normandy, Tuscany, and the Black Sea basin, it had moderate winters and fertile soils; its vast marshes and rivers provided countless wildfowl and fish. Once a week a chicken farmer from Elk Grove arrived in his truck with frying and roasting chickens and that rare kind of eggs whose yolks were dark orange from chickens ranging free and eating mixed grains from the fields. We always had fresh vegetables and fruits from the cornucopia of the Valley brought to our door by the truck farmers who circulated regularly through the neighborhood bringing many varieties of peaches, nectarines, cherries, apricots, plums, melons, pole beans, squash, lettuces, tomatoes. We had an old orange tree in our backyard that produced six lug boxes of navel oranges each winter to carry us through until the spring and summer fruits ripened on our peach and apricot trees.

My father and mother both loved cooking, and I learned to cook at an early age. One of the few happy memories I have of my early childhood is being with my mother in the kitchen doing little things to help her make cakes and cookies, and stirring sauces as they simmered. When I went away to college and brought friends home on the weekend, my mother would lay out her damask, fine silverware, and Lenox china. She spread the table for my ravenous friends with heaps of fresh prawns and cracked crab, tomatoes grown in our backyard, stuffed with Bay shrimp from the Farmers' Market, potato salad, warm sourdough from a bakery down the street, and one of her rich buttery cakes—devil's food or banana nut.

Despite the many delicious things she cooked and her careful attention to table setting and presentation, there is a strange note of asceticism about my mother's approach to meals, different from the sensual indulgence that characterized my father's cooking. Her kitchen is elaborately delineated, every imaginable size of pot and utensil in an exactly determined place, three complete sets of dishes and flatware—an everyday set, china from their wedding for sit-down dinners, and gold-rimmed Lenox for really fancy occasions—well-stocked staples and spices, liquor cabinet, drawers of well-ordered recipe books and recipe files. Unlike Great-Grandmother Lucy's and Grandmother Matilda's kitchens, with comfortable padded benches in cozy alcoves, fragrant stews and soups and coffee always brewing on the stove, ours had a modern home-economics aseptic quality. Despite the tasty foods, the actual experience of sitting around the table to eat them in our little dining nook was always physically uncomfortable for me.

I imagine my mother's ascetic order was her way of coping with the tragic loss of her mother Rose just before her thirteenth birthday. She was unexpectedly thrown into the role of homemaker from then until my father died sixty-five years later, with a good part of her life devoted to preparing three meals a day. After my father died, she began to cook meals only on the few occasions when she invites old friends or when I visit with my family. Otherwise, she eats boxed cereal, frozen prepared meals, or simple soups and salads. She tells me that she has no interest at all in cooking for herself.

My father typically devoted his rare days off construction jobs to outdoor barbecuing and creating new dishes in the kitchen with fresh catches of game or fish. But like the chef in a three-star restaurant, he devoted himself to elaborately, experimentally designed "main" dishes, for which my mother, like a line-chef, would spend the day behind the scenes preparing supplementary *hors d'oeuvres,* vegetables, salads, potatoes, and dessert. He once concocted a recipe for pheasant stew that earned an award and was published in *Sunset* magazine's *Chefs of the West.* Because he always downed a few drinks while he was cooking, my father would sometimes turn so hostile by dinner that my stomach was too upset to enjoy the food.

I got an outsider's viewpoint on the strangeness of this wild-west world, which I had taken as natural, when my first mother-in-law came with us to Sacramento in 1973 for Thanksgiving. She had emigrated as a young girl with her family from Minsk to the lower East Side of Manhattan and had spent her entire life in the heart of the city. As was his custom, my father went out hunting one day and managed to bring down two pheasants. She got to witness him cleaning and feathering them, and cooking them in his special way for dinner. She blushed like Lady Chatterly swept away by this rough gameskeeper who would dare venture out into the wilds with his gun to bag food for her.

Despite the treasure of raw materials, ours was not yet "California cuisine." It would take an Alice Waters and other chefs and food artisans to recognize the untapped tasting delights of the fecund California ecosystem within which I was raised. Chez Panisse in Berkeley became the clearinghouse of a style of cooking with techniques aimed at heightening the natural flavors lurking in this cornucopia, instead of losing them in overcooking or heavy sauces. It saved from extinction a network of many small suppliers of fruits, vegetables, dairy, meat, fowl, and fish, and created the market for many new entrepreneurs.

By education, religion, and the economy, we are imperceptibly drawn so far into the realm of abstract ideas and fantasies that we become incapable of noticing that tomatoes and peaches are tasting more like cardboard, there are far fewer kinds of butterflies in our gardens, the color of the air is getting browner, people are driving more violently, and our children and lovers are longing for contact.

When a young Wilhelm Reich was studying in Vienna with Freud in the 1920s, he was also interning as a physician treating the enormous population of poor immigrant workers living on the outskirts of the city in conditions reminiscent of my father's pipeline workers. Reich's experiences with these families made him realize that it was bourgeois folly to think of turning exclusively to psychoanalysis to effect a more humane society when so many people were crowded into hovels, physical and sexual abuse were rampant, women were subjected to men, and vast numbers of people had no decent health care. In the face of this situation, Reich created a synthesis of Freud's emphasis on healing intrapsychic conflict and Karl Marx's emphasis on improving the conditions of everyday work. He conceived of a two-pronged revolution: Socialist politics would work to ensure that the population had sufficient food, housing, medical care, and education. Individual psychoanalysis would deal with the inner barriers to intimacy and creative work.

His fundamental argument is that for one to develop a strong sense of self capable of standing on one's own thoughtfulness, one needs a highly developed familiarity with bodily sensations, both pleasurable and painful. One who lacks such a foundation, as I did throughout much of my life, is cast about either by imaginary inner voices whose origins are obscure, or the external voices of authorities. I found an accurate account of my long years of being held sway by religious authorities in his book *The Mass Psychology of Fascism,* where Reich argues that the dissociation from bodily sensations fostered by German Christianity created adults who had no solid core of stability to help them withstand Hitler's genius for mass manipulation. In a more general way, his arguments imply that adults who are untethered from an organic sense of self and one's basic desires are easy prey to the pulls of the media and charismatic individuals.

✧

In the Old Worlds, resting places along journeys were marked by sacred objects: the strings of chapels throughout Europe along the pilgrimage routes to San Juan de Campostela, stupas in the Himalayas, temples and shrines in the forests and hills of China and Japan. People traveling long and arduous routes paused in those places which, while providing food and drink, reminded them of the deeper purpose of their efforts.

Such places of roadside refreshment once held a critical place in the driving life of the Valley. When I first traveled to the East Coast in the 1950s, I was struck by how much closer the towns were, and how Howard Johnsons stood out as the singular road stops on the few freeways before the interstates began to proliferate. In the Valley, by contrast, distances between towns were longer and more empty. Driving in the summer heat without air conditioning made roadside stands even more important than they are now, when the automobiles themselves are more comfortable than the sterile places of rest. During the hot months, I thirsted for the next Giant Orange, a chain of roadside stands shaped like oranges, scattered every twenty miles or so throughout the Valley. They made a drink called a gremlin, which consisted of pure orange juice, frozen then pulverized. On the few days of the summer when they were in season, you could get a fresh lime gremlin, the most delicious of all. A row of small signs signaled their approach as you drove along Highway 99 south towards Stockton or up towards Williams. "Slurpies" from 7-Eleven and their like are but pale shadows of this drink, mainly sugar water stripped of the layers of fresh tastes embedded in the sensuous pulps.

The Nut Tree was the oasis of my childhood journeys. Interstate 80 cuts just south of what was then a vast sea of almond, walnut, peach, and apricot orchards stretching north for a hundred miles along the westernmost flats of the Valley at the base of the Pacific Coast Range, much of it now scraped of the rich topsoil and leveled for housing and industrial real estate ventures. The Nut Tree was originally a small roadside stand built on the Harbison Farm in 1922 by Bunny Power and Helen Harbison, newlywed farmers who had just graduated from what was then called The University Farm in Davis. The business took its name from the gigantic black walnut tree around which its overhanging roof was built. Soon the Powers opened a small restaurant in the back of the stand where they served up freshly cooked farm food—meatloaf, fried chicken, mashed potatoes, big loaves of bread hot from the oven, hunks of newly churned butter, hot chocolate, peach pies, and nut breads.

Our stops in that cozy place at a big family table were more than relaxing; they provided the rare kinds of refreshing moment where the pleasures of eating and drinking were intense enough to draw our family out of our nitpickings. I imagined something similar happened at the old chapels and inns along pilgrimage routes, places of recollection. We could forget the rigors of the interminable drives along the old two-lane highways in our cigarette-smoke-filled car, and my father's chronic grouchiness. The tastes of the nut breads made of local almonds and walnuts, real butter made from cows in the back pasture, and freshly milled flour all lingered pleasantly in the mouth, not needing to be washed down immediately by a Mountain Dew or Diet Pepsi. The complex nuanced flavors of the peaches and tomatoes enticed one to keep tasting as long as possible, as do the great wines of Burgundy. Their intensities interrupted, at least for a short moment, the exhausting onslaught of the all-too-familiar inner and outer chatter.

The archaic Nut Tree has remained a nostalgic fixture in my dreams throughout the long haul of my life, a place of meeting between the hermetic world of Sacramento and the hurly burly of the San Francisco Bay where I eventually settled. It marked a transition between the dry Valley heat and the wet fogs of the Pacific, a quiet refuge where you didn't feel the bumpy road and hear its roars. When I was beset with my divorces or betrayals, resentments about my upbringing, or doubts about the direction of my life, the Nut Tree would appear in my night dreams—I would be meeting with family or demons or angels over the homemade bread and soup to find some peaceful resolution. I could meet there and talk quietly with my parents even when my life had drifted so far away from theirs.

The textured warm sensuality of the old dining room became for me a dream symbol of how we might think together more creatively and effectively about how to resolve the enormous challenges that face us. Those times at the Nut Tree before the post-war boom were among the earliest hints I got of a life that was based on a more serious attention to the material world and to the body—the primeval structures of this world—its pleasures more satisfying than the calculating rationalities and trivial conventions that governed the world I grew up in. Those tastes gave me a hint of a more sensual, kinder, and more tolerant life than I felt around me in the narrow-minded attitudes of the Valley.

Like all the old farms in the Valley, the soul of Nut Tree was lost, first expanding into a chrome and glass restaurant. They hired cooks and standardized the memorized family recipes for breads, pies, and stews to the extent that they came to taste like anything you could buy at Denny's or Safeway. They added a kids' playground with a narrow-gauge railway, expanded the parking lot into the largest one between San Francisco and Sacramento, built a small airport and a minor-league baseball stadium. They kept adding wings to the restaurant until it could seat about five hundred people. When they opened The Coffee Tree on the opposite side of the freeway, you knew that the devil had won the bargain. The original had been named for the black walnut tree right outside the door; you would have to travel a long way from here to find a real coffee tree. The new popular dessert was pineapple marshmallow cake in which there was not a single local ingredient. All special places were being transformed into Cartesian abstract spaces where you could buy anything from anywhere anytime. Near the end, the owners added an enormous façade to protect its diners from the roar of the interstate, which stood alone for ten years after the restaurant itself was demolished, until in 2004 it also came down, leaving only the vacant parking lot. All the action is across the way at the Nut Tree Outlet Mall, just like every other outlet mall from here to Waco, Texas. The sense of resting for a while in a special place, where the Putah Creek comes down from the Coast Range into the great wetlands where the Patwin and Miwok villages used to be, the smells and tastes that existed nowhere else, are all gone, swallowed up in noise, exhaust, and tract houses.

The Eden Development Group has proposed to the City of Vacaville an ambitious plan for a virtual Nut Tree city, including a luxury hotel, two restaurants, a main street with 225,000 square feet of retail space, and 640,000 square feet of office buildings, five hundred apartments, and two championship golf courses. The developers are quoted as thinking of themselves as idealists who say: "We would want to bring back the Nut Tree as it was in the early days. This would be 'California.' There would be nothing phony about it at all."

5

Bad Manners

RICHARD RODRIGUEZ WRITES OF HIS SACRAMENTO UPBRINGING: "My mother and father (with immigrant pragmatism) assumed the American tongue would reinvent their children."[5] Proper English grammar and pronunciation seemed like a key to acceptance by the community. Rules of etiquette played a similar role in assimilation. The reinvention of American children could not be achieved without education in proper manners. And yet, there is the strange phenomenon that America stands out in the world for its lack of gentility.

In 2002, a research group funded by the Pew Trust released a study entitled "Aggravating Circumstances: A Status Report on Rudeness in America." It found that 80 percent of the adults surveyed believed that lack of respect and courtesy is a serious problem in American society, manifested in various social settings. The president of the group reports: "Lack of manners for Americans is not whether you confuse the salad fork for the dinner fork. It is about the daily assault of selfish, inconsiderate behavior that gets under their skin on the highways, in the office, on TV, in stores and the myriad other settings where they encounter fellow Americans."[6]

During most of my childhood, my family was just struggling to survive. The house my father built was very small, squeezed by the limits of the narrow lot that my grandfather had owned. There were two bedrooms, one bathroom, a small dining room, and a very small den, which was soon converted into a bedroom when my mother's father moved in with us after his clothing store closed. After World War II ended and my father began to make more money in the booming California heavy construction industry, the first thing that changed in our house was table-wear. My parents bought a full set of sterling flatware engraved with "J," gold-edged Lenox china, fine damask, and Swedish crystal. They purchased an expensive membership in the Del Paso Country Club. When old friends came for dinner, we now crowded into our tiny dining room around the table elaborately set according to the rules prescribed by Emily Post, a new reference book in our house shelved next to the Bible.

"Etiquette" came to represent the complex set of mysterious rules that were required of us if we were to move out of the lower working class into the solid middle. Those arcane procedures seemed to govern every aspect of social behavior: the setting of the table and the appropriate moves to be made when sitting there, the proper kinds of clothing for different occasions, the correct forms of address, formats of letters, postures and gestures, and who knows what else. Etiquette was for my parents what English was for their forebears, a fully formed, complex, unknown system that had to be learned with great difficulty, and then always practiced with a trace of awkwardness. My parents seemed always to be struggling to figure out what the rules were and how to implement them if they were to continue to move upwards in society. In that struggle, they always seemed to feel themselves as outsiders not really knowing what to do.

The first time I remember clearly becoming aware of "etiquette" as an agreed-upon, highly defined, and very complicated body of rules was in seventh grade just at the end of World War II. I had gone to public schools until the end of sixth grade, when my parents transferred me to a Catholic elementary school. Like most kids finding themselves at that erotically charged age in a totally strange community, I felt very uncomfortable with boys and girls who had known each other for at least six years. They were all Catholics, mostly from lower working-class families whose grandparents, like mine, had been born in the Old World. A few weeks into the school year, I received an invitation in the mail to a Halloween party at one of the girls' houses. It was the ordinary kind of kid's invitation you buy in drugstores, a playful design of pumpkins and goblins with blanks filled in with the date and time of the party. I could feel the anxiety in my mother as she seemed to be bracing herself for a very important social occasion requiring standards that were mysterious to her. The stakes seemed higher than one might expect. She got out her Emily Post to consult the section on responses to invitations. Because there were no directions for pubescent Halloween parties, she followed its instructions for replies to invitations for weddings, formal parties, and teas, having me painstakingly copy in black India ink this prescribed reply on the required blank ivory card:

> Donald Hanlon Johnson accepts with pleasure your
> invitation to a Halloween party on October Thirty-First,
> Nineteen Hundred and Forty-Six,
> at Twelve Hundred and One "K" Street
> from Seven to Nine O'clock Post Meridian.

Then she took me to Weinstock and Lubin's Department Store, where I was fitted out in a double-breasted tan linen suit, a white shirt with French cuffs, a tie, and wing-tip leather shoes. I arrived for the party in a small modest house like ours where the boys and girls, all easily familiar with each other, were wearing the casual clothes you might expect. I have a photograph of me standing there looking like a newly arrived immigrant on Ellis Island in my ill-fitting suit and bewildered facial expression. I sensed that the formal reply and my dress had provoked some gossip about my weirdness.

Wilhelm Reich's *The Mass Psychology of Fascism,* an analysis of how Hitler could rise to power in a highly civilized German society, links servile attitudes towards etiquette with the success of fascism. He argues that education in conventionality—an obsession with "re-invention"—produces a character that habitually and automatically looks outside the self for direction. If these attitudes are effectively broadcast to the point where they seize hold of the imagination of the masses, they succeed in producing a self-defeating identification of the masses with oppressive power. Longing for inclusion in a world whose rules elude them, conditioned to strive to be something they do not understand, people lose contact both with their own sense of self-direction as well as their more humane feelings for others.

> At first it is only the idea of being like one's superior that stirs the mind of the employee or the official, but gradually, owing to his pressing material dependence, his whole person is refashioned in line with the ruling class. ... He lives in materially reduced circumstances, but assumes gentlemanly postures on the surface, often to a ridiculous degree. He eats poorly and insufficiently, but attaches great importance to a "decent suit of clothes." A silk hat and dress coat become the material symbol of this character structure.[7]

Vast numbers of clear-thinking and good-hearted Germans could see the horrors coming but were unable to rally enough strength to stop them because, Reich argues, they made the fatal mistake that the masses could be motivated by "reason," when in fact they were being swept away by the costumes, music, symbols, and hypnotic cadences of Hitler's speeches playing on primal fears.

> The revolutionary movement also failed to appreciate the importance of the seemingly irrelevant everyday

habits, indeed, very often turned them to bad account. The lower middle-class bedroom suite, which the "rabble" buys as soon as he has the means, even if he is otherwise revolutionary minded; the consequent suppression of the wife, even if he is a Communist; the "decent" suit of clothes for Sunday; "proper" dance steps and a thousand other "banalities," have an incomparably greater reactionary influence when repeated day after day than thousands of revolutionary rallies and leaflets can ever hope to counterbalance. Narrow conservative life exercises a continuous influence, penetrates every facet of everyday life ... [8]

✧

My grandparents' house had an Old World feel, permeated with smells of coffee sitting all day on the heater, meatballs and soups always simmering on the stove, casual eating of ample amounts of food, prepared for the hard-working men. I don't remember "places being set" or any talk of propriety. There was a comfortable informality, with meals usually being taken at a cozy nook in the kitchen. And yet, I do not remember vulgarity or rudeness in that setting.

The difference between the aura of meals in my grandparents' house and our own is accurately described by the late Pierre Bourdieu:

> In opposition to the free-and-easy working-class meal, the bourgeoisie is concerned to eat with all due form. Form is first of all a matter of rhythm, which implies expectations, pauses, restraints; waiting until the last person served has started to eat, taking modest helpings, not appearing over-eager. A strict sequence is observed. ...[9]

Despite my parents' slow upward move into the comfortable middle class, and the amount of money they spent traveling the world, buying fine clothes, eating excellent food served on an increasing array of fine dinnerware, and financing my college education, they remained squeezed into a small house in an increasingly depressed and crime-ridden neighborhood for forty years.

After I graduated from college, by then thoroughly schooled in Emily Post, I entered the Jesuit novitiate to begin my studies for the priesthood and the long years of initiation into the religious order. Each Saturday morning, Father Joe Meehan, a dry-humored, husky, San Francisco Irish priest who would have done well as a fire chief or Democratic ward boss, would enter our lecture hall, draw out a large white linen napkin, a set of silverware, plates, delicate cups, and crystal, and order them properly on the desk in front of him. He pursed his lips as he seated himself daintily, then proceeded to give us lessons on how to use the utensils—the proper glasses for red and white wine, how to wipe excess food from one's lips and dispose of olive pits, how to stifle possible burps and farts—all in good Irish wit. I was puzzled about why we, who were devoting our lives to becoming mystics and missionaries charged by the Pope with bringing the message of Jesus to the furthest reaches of the world, were having these classes in secular niceties. It was only much later that I came to realize that we were being educated to sit among the upper classes who funded our vast networks of high schools and universities. Most Jesuits, like myself, came from working-class families. Their parents, however, had not been as concerned as mine about the manners of the upper classes. Learning the language of elegant tables was a missionary strategy every bit as important as learning the language of the country in which one was living. A burping bumpkin with food hanging from his chin would hardly be effective in his mission to insinuate Christian doctrine into the homes of power and wealth.

My son seems to have gone through etiquette stages of development. He hears from our English immigrant neighbors with three children how much looser manners are here in California. From other Japanese friends with two boys who live nearby, and his own visit to Japan, he knows that manners there are different from here and England. He knows, for example, that Japanese pride themselves on developing lip muscles to slurp soba with a potent sound. He delights in the sucking concerts at Tokyo noodle counters, and he has watched our friends slurp. He been to France and Italy and knows that Europeans twirl their pasta around a fork with the help of a large spoon before they bring it quietly into the mouth. As we were eating dinner together at home recently he said to me, "I never want to live in England." "Why is that?" I asked. "They have too strict manners," he replied. "I want to live in Japan where they slurp." He continues, impishly putting his finger in his nose then into his mouth, "Would they like this in England, Dad?" "How about this?"—letting out a huge burp, then a fart. "Would grandma like it if I did this?"—getting up and running boisterously around the table.

My son's behavior is not accurately described as animal in nature, or as crudely material. It is in fact uniquely human, saturated with trickster humor, cross-cultural insight, and devices cleverly designed to upset his grandmothers, along with adult guests who appear in his eyes to be a little too serious. This is not the behavior of our pet dog. My concern as a father is not to abstract him from his body, but to help him gain respect for others, a sense of their needs as well as his own. My work is to create a more pleasurable social situation where he is not disrupting our meals by commandeering all the attention, or by emitting offensive odors and sounds. In that sense, learning manners is like learning the rules of soccer, playing a musical instrument, or dancing—practices that make human interaction more pleasurable. These strategies do not need to have the primary aim of making one less animal or bodily, but less aggressive and narcissistic.

The Swiss sociologist Norbert Elias is the author of one of the most extensive historical analyses of manners, which he situates at the heart of what he calls "the civilizing process." He argues that the rules of etiquette are like the rules of dance—what he calls "figurations," the creative forms that shape particular communities out of many individuals:

> One should think of a mazurka, a minuet, a polonaise, a tango, or rock 'n' roll. The image of the mobile figurations of interdependent people on a dance floor perhaps makes it easier to imagine states, cities, families, and also capitalist, communist, and feudal systems as figurations. By using this concept we can eliminate the antithesis, resting finally on different values and ideals, immanent today in the use of the words "individual" and "society." One can certainly speak of a dance in general, but no one will imagine dance as a structure outside the individual or as a mere abstraction. The same dance figurations can certainly be danced by different people; but without a plurality of reciprocally oriented and dependent individuals, there is no dance.[10]

Like social dances, manners can make people feel clumsy and ill at ease, generate envy of their betters, enhance their fun, lead to wonderfully erotic encounters, or even end up in brawls. I had trouble with both social dances and manners, always feeling like I had five

thumbs and sprained ankles. For me and many of my contemporaries, the 1960s were among other things a rebellion against the
figurations of the previous generation, both their etiquette and social
dances. I found myself revelling in free-form rock-and-roll and table
manners. The first time I took LSD, I indulged in the ecstatic pleasure of devouring a wonderful meal like a dog, shoveling the food in
my mouth with my bare hands, slurping, smearing the juices over my
face. I let my hair grow unkempt, wore shaggy clothes, belched and
farted at will. When I paid my first visit to Esalen Institute in Big Sur
at that time, I encountered the Fritz Perls Gestalt community, who
believed that manners were inauthentic. If you said "good morning"
to someone, he looked at you with a cold stare, letting you know
what a phony he thought you were. I felt as awkward and uncomfortable at Esalen in those years as I did at the seventh-grade Halloween
party. It was the beginning of a new "figuration" in America that
might be called the "do-your-own-thing" figuration, which has polluted our social life, leaving us with insensitive drivers, loud babblers
in small restaurants, and hikers in the back country peeing directly
in the clear streams, leaving toilet paper beside the lupine, polluting
the majestic sounds of the winds with their cell phones.

✧

Religion has a central role in how a culture incorporates etiquette. The feel of mannerly behavior in Kyoto is very different
from that in Paris.

Christianity has conflated etiquette and moral virtue to the point
that they are often mistaken for each other. The Greek term for
ethics, $\varepsilon\theta o\varsigma$, meant customs, the way a community organized itself, Elias's "figurations." Aristotle's *Ethics* argued that the study of
customs was important to determine which particular practices led
to what he defined as the shared goal of all human activity, happiness, and how those practices might be refined. In that original

sense, etiquette was linked with gentlemanly satisfactions rooted in a harmonious (patriarchal, of course) community.

In the thirteenth century, Thomas Aquinas and a host of medieval theologians transformed Aristotle's goal of creating satisfying humane intercourse into the pursuit of the salvation of one's eternal soul created by a God who laid down laws defining goodness and its pursuit. They created a synthesis of classical Greek ethical philosophy and the complex rules found in the ancient Christian Penitentials, arcane and little-known documents that detail every possible sin and the conditions for its forgiveness.

My guess is that few laymen have any sense that this weird strain of reasoning about human foibles exists in the dark halls of the monasteries and the Vatican. The early Penitentials were the first attempts to spell out the complexities of sin, their degrees of evil, and the specific penances that would lead to their forgiveness. As literary texts, they bear more similarity to the writings of Baudelaire and de Sade than to the more angelic philosophical tracts. In Bosch-like fantasy, they concoct in bizarre detail any possible sin that one might commit in the wildest flights of desire. In a not atypical passage, for example, an early Irish monk wrote:

> Anyone who eats the flesh of a horse, or drinks the blood or urine of an animal, does penance for three years and a half. Anyone who drinks liquid in which there is a dead mouse does seven days' penance therefor. Anyone who drinks or eats the leavings of a mouse does penance for a day and a night. Theodore says that although food be touched by the hand of one polluted or by dog, cat, mouse, or unclean animal that drinks blood, this does no harm.[11]

One might think that this prescription had more to do with manners than with morality: disgusting behavior, not to be done in public. But these prescriptions typically enter a realm where the disgusting is elided with the morally reprehensible: "He who sins with a beast shall do penance for a year; if by himself, for three 40-day periods; if he has clerical rank, a year; a boy of fifteen years, forty days. He who defiles his mother shall do penance for three years with perpetual exile."[12]

Here you can see the dubious conflations of radically different kinds of behavior (sex with sheep and with one's mother) that have something to do with the sad state of morality of priests and bishops exposed in recent years. It is as if the cataloguing of thousands of fantasy trees obscured the forest of love and respect.

The transformation from the humane view of Aristotle to the theological view of early Christian scholasticism left intrinsic contradictions. On the one hand, Jesus's discourses, like those of the Buddha and Lao Tse, emphasized love and care for other people. In that sense, etiquette clearly bears on morality inasmuch as its rules are concerned with embodying intentions of kindness and respect in actual behavior, not simply in good thoughts. Despite that foundational message, the overwhelming emphasis in the Catholic moral theology in which I was indoctrinated was not on nurturing the human community, but on obeying the imagined dictates of God, often in behaviors that have no discernible relationship to the well-being of other human beings.

When I was in the final stages of my Jesuit initiation, about to be ordained with the powers to hear confessions, our most important preparatory course was in moral theology. It was an infamous course, talked about for years during our preparatory training, with covert references to its kinky sexual content. Like the ancient Penitentials, the course indeed had a tone of surreal and twisted sexual fantasy. Although we dealt with all the sins proscribed by the Ten Commandments and the six special commandments of the Roman Church, the emphasis was on "sins of the flesh." We discussed every possible kind of sexual activity, imaginable orifice, with large and small animals as well as different kinds of humans. Our textbook, used in Catholic seminaries throughout the world, was the up-to-date version of the Penitentials. Its author was a German Capuchin Friar Heribert Jone, the text translated and "adapted to the laws and customs of the United States of America" by Friar Urban Adelman in 1963. We examined intricacies of masturbation skirted in high-school religion classes: It is alright for a man, wrote Friar Jone,

> ... to wash, go swimming, riding, etc. even though one foresees that due to one's particular excitability in this regard, pollution will follow. Similarly, it is lawful to seek relief from itching in the sex organs, provided the irritation is not the result of superfluous semen or ardent passion. In case one doubts about the cause of the itching he may relieve it. It is likewise lawful in case of slight itching if only slight sexual stimulation is experienced therefrom.[13]

Friar Jone prided himself on a modernist sensibility in finally having arrived at a non-sexist definition of "pollution" as "complete sexual satisfaction obtained by some form of self-stimulation." He boasts of his formulation: "By evading reference to 'semination' our definition evades the various controversies concerning the specific difference of this sin in men, women, eunuchs, and those who have not reached the age of puberty, since only men are capable of secreting semen in the proper sense of the word."

The argument justifying these weird imaginings was that since we were about to enter the dark confessional to hear the full catalogue of human waywardness, we had to be prepared to diagnose every imaginable sin, and judge its degree of seriousness to determine the appropriate penance. And the sins that most concerned the "Fathers of the Church" were masturbation and various forms of intercourse. Only very late in the history of moral theology did sins like social justice and inflicting state-sanctioned torture begin to gain attention, and they remain on the margins of Christian moral concerns today.

By striking contrast, Buddhist, Taoist, and Hindu discourses about erotic behavior are more in the realm of etiquette and con- figurations: how to increase the intensity of pleasure and mystical insight. There are ample teachings about how to approach one's own body and one's partners, various kinds of touch to a variety of bodily surfaces and orifices to evoke ranges of delight, breathing practices for engaging and intensifying excitement, specific directions for the use of flowers, perfumes, oils, music, and dress. The rules here, like good table manners, are about enhancing the pleasures of congress. In China and India, the study of the figurations of human behavior had to do with the fullest development of the human community, allowing the ultimate flowering of its capacities of pleasure and wisdom.

✧

From the dinner table and the bedroom to the cells of political torture and fields of slaughter.

The dedication page of Norbert Elias's analysis of the so-called civilizing process is haunting:

> Dedicated to the Memory of My Parents
> Hermann Elias, d. Breslau 1940
> Sophie Elias, d. Auschwitz 1941 (?)

I cannot believe it was written without deliberate and grief-stricken irony that the behaviors, which he is about to describe so dispassionately in the ensuing volumes, identified as the marks of high civilization, characterized the very men who supervised the murder of his parents.

Natural tendencies towards humane behaviors can indeed find in manners a help towards their flowering, but such behaviors are by no means guaranteed by mastering the manners themselves. In our own generations, we have seen masters of etiquette engineer extreme horrors. The chilling film *Closetland* gives an accurate fictional portrayal of what typically happens in educated and skilled political torture. With Philip Glass's haunting music in the background, Alan Rickman plays the torturer of a young female author of children's fantasy books who is charged with using metaphors to criticize an anonymous regime. He is elegantly dressed in a gray suit, white shirt, and tie, and exhibits impeccable manners, punctuated by the briefest blow here, a sudden piercing there, an electrode quickly shoved into the woman's orifices—but without giving up for more than a moment his exterior graciousness. His exquisite refinement is what makes the physical pain of the torture even more horrible. This, and countless real instances like it throughout the world, are not the acts of individuals out of control in bloodlust, but highly educated manifestations of civilized, even scientific reason. Like the Holocaust and Abu Ghraib, this kind of behavior requires oversight by a sophisticated culture of chemists and biologists, architectural and transportation engineers, psychiatrists, physicians, and the kinds of professionals who staff our tax-supported School of the Americas in Georgia, the Harvard of schools for political torturers from favored allies around the world.

Focus on minute rules of behavior can distract the gentleman or woman, and the communities under their sway, from the reasons for the rules—the nurturance of the human community. Like the pedophiliac priest and his protector bishop schooled in the subtleties of Heribert Jone, well-mannered government, military, and global corporate executives have learned to shut off their feelings for the humans they are abusing, let alone the Earth that supports us, no matter how much they confess, apologize, or shed tears of seeming grief.

6

The Missionary Position

I N THE BEGINNING WAS THE WORD, and the Word was with God, and the Word was God. And the Word was made flesh—*Et Verbum caro factum est*—and dwelt among us.

From the time I was a child well until adulthood when the Vatican Council expunged the passage from the reformed liturgy, I heard the priest intone that phrase from the prologue of John's Gospel at mass every Sunday and often during weekday masses. At the first hint of the priest's *"Et,"* a rustle swept through the church as we fell on our knees in special reverence for the founding moment of Christianity, the core of our belief, the incarnation in an embryo in a woman's womb of an indescribable creative spirit. That phrase was repeated and glossed on in every theological commentary through the centuries: a vast, inaccessible, and unformed Something first condensed itself into language and that language took on perceivable shapes.

Even though there have always been vigorous anti-intellectual currents within Christianity, the very earliest theologians argued that the language which revealed the otherwise Unknowable was at its most basic level present in the natural patterns of order in earth and cosmos. Albert the Great, Thomas Aquinas, Roger and Francis Bacon, Leonardo da Vinci, and Pierre Teilhard de Chardin are only a few among the many who argued that because everything is a manifestation of the divine mind, any inquiry into the structures of reality can lead one closer to glimpses of that mind itself. Those scientists who would decipher the syntax of stars and cells were considered to be full-fledged partners in the theological venture.

Second in revelatory meaning to physical creation was human history itself, where theologians looked to find the divine code—most especially, but not exclusively, in the history recorded in the Scriptures. In this view, the climax of that history occurs in the life and death of Jesus, brought to its unexpected conclusion in the resurrection of his body—the promise, argues Paul, of the transformation of our bodies from the meaningless hunks of meat *(sarx)* into the luminous flesh like that enjoyed by yogis, taoists, and other spiritual practitioners throughout history. This concentration on the human body as the special place where the divine language can be deciphered would take hold in the Renaissance, when Leonardo and Vesalius initiated the long history of intricate studies of the fibers and cells of our being, and the artists of Florence and the Lowlands put onto canvas the radiance of the human form. The human body, in this view, is our most intimate access to understanding the crafts of the divine. Because of its unique capacities for knowing and loving, it reveals the inner nature of divine reality in ways that cannot be shown by nature alone.

The divine, words, and the human body: a trinity whose puzzles continued to remain at the core of my life's work, even when I had ceased to count myself among the believers. How can we speak about things that are most meaningful to us instead of trivial nonsense? How can those words truly reflect the soil and blood from which they arise when language seems so far from reality? The belief that a God inexpressible in language and inaccessible to the human mind and senses was to be found in the natural realities of cosmos, history, and the body would be layered over by centuries of moralisms and nit-picking theological speculations. But for serious theologians, among whom I spent my adolescence and early adulthood, it remained the soul of belief.

My childhood indoctrination into the ancient spiritual practice of looking deeply into the physical world for revelations of divinity accounts for my lifelong interest in looking to the changing California landscape and the bodily experience of that landscape for clues to the deeper realities of our present human situation. That early catechetical seed would be nourished in later adulthood by studies of esoteric strands of Christian mysticism that emphasized bodily transformation; doctoral studies focused on phenomenological philosophy; and finally, an adult life given to the study and practice of various methods of exploring bodily experience.

✧

It is impossible to understand the peculiar irrationalities of our post-9/11 world without grasping the particular ways that religious teaching shapes social consciousness. Manifest Destiny, the virulent repressions of sexuality, the conflicts surrounding issues about how far the State can intrude on human life by abortion, capital punishment, and war—these escape rational argument because the primal sources of such beliefs lie in unquestioned religious faith.

Like countless other Americans, I was raised with the conviction that I belonged to a divinely chosen community whose carefully defined dogmas were crucial for the well-being of those human beings who had never heard of these dogmas; and even more crucial for those who knew of them but refused to accept them. From the time of my earliest catechism classes, I became convinced that the most important task of my life was to spread these truths among as many people as I could during my lifetime. It is hard to imagine that even as a child, I believed that I had a better grasp of the meaning of life than my non-Catholic father. That zealous sense of superiority which I held for nearly half my life gives me an intimate sense of the conflicts raging today among communities fired by such a sense, most obviously Christian and Islamic ideologues, but also their secular equivalents.

Missionary idealism is not simply a mental construct, but an embodied stance towards life. You can see it in the eyes of the zealot. When he seems to be looking at you straight in the eye, he is ever so slightly out of focus, thinking of his next move to capture your allegiance. You might notice that his words seem to flow on undeterred by your responses; you might hear in his voice an insistent resonance whose musicality has a repetitive drone. No matter how sensitive and kind he is, the missionary is always seeking to be on top where he can pour the seeds of truth into one who, by dint of lacking these truths, is cajoled into lying passively on the bottom.

That energetic, wildly hopeful missionary attitude came to me through the small Irish strand in my mother's family.

Unlike nearby San Francisco with its two cathedrals—Episcopal Grace crowning Nob Hill and Catholic St. Mary's on Cathedral Hill—and cities in farming regions in older parts of the world where spires of churches, mosques, and temples mark the horizons from afar, the Valley towns gave few hints of religion. A dramatic exception was the Cathedral of the Blessed Sacrament, our parish church. Up until the 1950s, as you approached Sacramento from the west on the causeway from Davis, all that would appear against the distant backdrop of the Sierras, with the Sutter Buttes on your left, were the spire of the fifteen-story Elks Club, the cupolas of the Cathedral and Capitol Domes, and the art deco lines of the Tower Theater on Broadway. Our church's prominence on the skyline belied the fact that Roman Catholicism was but a small minority religion in the city.

Our Cathedral parish took in the central downtown area from the Sacramento riverfront and the railroad yards, where the farm workers and newly arrived immigrants managed to live crowded into tiny houses tucked next to the levees, out to 19th Street at the corner of our block. Just beyond that was St. Francis parish with its Mission-style church and school across from Sutter's Fort and the tiny Indian museum that displayed the only evidence I ever saw that the Valley had been settled and cultivated long before the Europeans arrived.

When I read the memoirs of this same period in Sacramento by Richard Rodriguez, whose family had come from Mexico, I am struck by the more home-like nature of his Catholicism: statues of Mary and the saints, votive candles, grace before meals, prayers before bed, often a family rosary, a grandmother who was openly devout and prayerful. By contrast, the Catholicism of my grandfather Joe and my mother was a lonely and quiet affair dissociated from day-to-day home life: no grace, no statues, no mention of religious matters. Our Catholicism was about the salvation of an essentially lonely soul.

In classic Catholic theology, the family, the body, and the Earth are but ephemeral realities, into which the individual immortal soul is inserted for but a miniscule portion of its eternal existence. The real action is the soul's journey towards union with God or eternal damnation. Although Catholic moral rules require the nurturing of family life, devotion to our loved ones must be put aside whenever there might be a question of danger to one's soul. From the earliest catechism instructions all the way through the most sophisticated Christian mystical texts, we were constantly embued with the implications of these words of Jesus: "Everyone who has given up home, brothers or sisters, father or mother, wife or children or property for my sake will receive many times as much and inherit everlasting life." (Matthew 19:29)

Jesuit spirituality, to which I devoted my young adulthood, trained me to be completely indifferent to the needs of family and

locality. Such a spirituality was crucial for a special forces that had
to be ready to go anywhere in the world at a moment's notice to
serve the interests of the Pope. A paradigm of virtue often mentioned in our Jesuit training was an instance in the life of St. Francis
Xavier when he was on his way to catch the ship that would take
him to Asia for the rest of his life. On the road from Rome to his
port of embarcation in Portugal, he saw his family estate on the
horizon and was prompted to visit them to say a last farewell. But
remembering those words of Jesus, he continued to the harbor,
never to see them again. And so with countless stories of spiritual
devotees throughout the ages around the planet and their secular
counterparts: Hindu renunciates, Islamic suicide bombers, Marxist
and Nazi youth who turned in their parents to authorities for de-
parting from orthodoxy.

I took to this spiritual teaching, finding it a welcome justification
for abandoning a family I found too depressing. I welcomed the
rule in our Jesuit seminaries that strictly limited visits with parents
to one Sunday a month for two hours, and forbade any gifts from
them. I used the biblical teaching, shored up in later years by secular psychoanalytic critique of parents, to justify an effective aban-
donment of my mother and father as they aged, rarely going home
to visit or to help out when they were sick or needed assistance
moving their belongings to a new house.

In accord with Roman policies about a frowned-upon "mixed"
marriage between a Catholic and a Protestant, my father and mother had been married in the priest's house next door to the Cathedral in a furtive ceremony. I wonder what it was like for them and
their families to have to be subjected to this covert ceremony, as
if they were minor criminals, doing something that had to be kept
secret rather than celebrated.

As is still the rule for mixed marriages, my father was required to sign a contract that any of their children would be baptized and *dad* raised Catholic. I found it something of a betrayal that my father signed my soul over to these priests, when I could see that he had little tolerance for all the picayune details of Catholic morality, particularly fish on Friday and Christmas Eve, and no contraceptives. Each Sunday, my mother, grandfather Joe, and I would walk to the Cathedral through Capitol Park. My father would stay in bed until we returned. On Fridays, when we were home he insisted on eating meat when my mother and I were required to have fish. If we went out to a restaurant, however, he always ordered fish. When I was a child, my mother's closest cousin, Bernard McMahon, married Lorna, a Presbyterian, "outside the Church," as theologians said. Because Catholics were forbidden to traffic with such sinners, my mother and I stopped seeing Bernard except for rare and very brief embarrassed encounters at social events.

The unfamilial cast of Irish Catholicism tainted our holidays. Following Scandinavian custom, we always celebrated Christmas on the Eve at Matilda and Jul's house with a big turkey dinner and Old Country specialities. Because Christmas Eve was a prescribed fastday for Catholics, my mother would bring a little tuna casserole covered with crispy potato chips to Matilda and Jul's house, which Grandpa Joe, my mother, and I would eat while everyone else was eating turkey and home-pickled pigs' feet, Jul's favorite holiday treat.

By contrast to the playful familial spirit of Christmas Eve, which I always looked forward to, mass at the quiet and cavernous Cathedral the next morning with my mother and Grandpa Joe was a sad affair.

My father's sister Charlotte was the first modern woman in our family. She joined the WAVES during World War II, and then enrolled in Heald's Business College and worked her way up into the ranks of skilled executive secretaries. At some point, to my mother's joy and her parents' consternation, she converted to Catholicism. Unlike other women in the family, she didn't marry early. As she approached thirty, everyone in the family worried that she was going to become an "old maid." She was rumored to be having an affair with her boss, the plant manager of the local Campbell's Soup Company, married and father of two boys. He divorced his wife, and they announced their marriage. Everyone in the family liked him and was relieved that Charlotte was finally getting married, except for my mother who foresaw the dilemmas ahead. Since he was divorced, the Church considered such a marriage an invalid charade and forbade Catholics to participate. The happiest memento I have of my father and his family is a portrait taken at Charlotte's wedding. My father, his mother Matilda (my grandfather Jul had died by then), and my aunts Gladys and Charlotte stand bursting with joy—the three women dressed in glistening silks and pearls, my grandmother wearing a lavishly flowered hat, my father handsome in a dark suit and silk tie. My mother and I are conspicuously absent, piously alone at home in accordance with Catholic rules.

When I married for the first time in my thirties, it was to a Jewish woman. One of the things that I found so surprisingly attractive about our life together was the familial character of Judaism; it was almost as if I married her, her children, and her family and community as much as her. It is hard to grasp the profound difference between a religion that puts primary emphasis on the salvation of an individual immortal soul and one that puts primary emphasis on the eternal community carried on by giving birth and raising children within the family. After some years away from Jewish rituals, I attended a Bat Mitzvah not long after 9/11 and was surprised to break into tears at the very first chant: this raucous booming community chanting these ancient hymns, sounding together, young girls, a contactful rabbi, the mothers and fathers right up there in places of prominence. Nothing could be more different from the lonely and divisive spirituality in which I was raised.

The Cathedral, where we worshipped, mirrored this sense of isolation. It felt too big, like a huge empty cavern, its pews for 3,200 people rarely more than a quarter filled, except on special occasions such as when Chicago's Cardinal Stritch came for a Eucharistic Congress. Greeted by kettle drums and trumpets augmenting the organ in the choir loft, he was impressive enough for the space in his ermine-trimmed shantung robes and red patent-leather shoes with diamond buckles. The sanctuary, several stairs up beyond the communion rail, was large enough to hold all the priests in the diocese and a large cadre of altar boys. The pulpit was high up on the distant right side, where pastor Father Renwald, tall, skinny, and bashful, preached in the thinnest of voices, quavering, barely able to reach us in the pew where we always sat, halfway down on the left. The choir was so far above us in its third-story loft that it was hard to hear their words. Catholicism felt like an eviscerated, almost ghostly religion, colored by Grandpa Joe's and my mother's personal sadness and the long-standing troubles of Ireland as well.

Unlike the older Catholic communities in Boston, New York, Charleston, and San Francisco where children of Catholic immigrants had been there long enough in large numbers to gain political and economic power, Valley Catholics were still on the frontier. We were few—a small community of poor Irish immigrants and the larger one of Mexican Americans. Our priests were mostly Irish-born missionaries, sent there to compete with mainstream Protestants, evangelicals, and charismatics for a foothold in a community that came there more for gold and farmland than for any religious motivation, unlike the refugees from religious persecution who first populated the Eastern seaboard. It was not until the 1960s that a native Sacramentan was ordained, a man who had been three years behind me in high school. Our Bishop Armstrong was a farmer from the Yakima Valley in Washington who seemed to have little taste for Roman royal trappings. When he would officiate at a holiday mass or confirmation, he would regularly slump down into his pillowed throne, wrapped in his purple silks and Chantilly lace, fall asleep and snore loudly. He lived in a sprawling and decaying old Victorian house on 21st and Capitol Avenue just two blocks from our house. Sometimes when I was coming home from grade school and I met him walking along in his food-stained and dandruff-dusted black suit and Roman collar, he would join me and ask how I was doing. He was a kind man.

When I entered third grade at Fremont, the State passed a law allowing "release-time" religious instruction. One day a week, the only three of us Catholics in the whole school would walk over to St. Francis for catechism, while the rest of our schoolmates thronged over to the Baptist Church, giving us jeers about our superstitious foreign religion. Franciscan Father John conducted the classes, the first man I ever had as a teacher, religious or secular. Somehow he didn't look the role of a priest. He was lean and muscular, a fair-haired blue-eyed Errol Flynn, with long hair always carefully arranged in a style close to what we then called a duck's tail. His voice was so mellow that he was always chosen to sing the high masses and special ritual chants. I remember almost nothing about our actual classes beyond his appearance, the lonely walks between there and Fremont, and the jibes of our classmates. He always seemed a little distracted, and eventually disappeared for reasons I never knew, though I guessed it had something to do with sex.

The many special rules required of us as Catholics alienated me from the kids in my neighborhood, accentuating my feelings of isolation. When I was invited to Friday night parties, I had to bring

bishop's office for permission to cross over the parish boundaries to attend St. Francis School for seventh and eighth grades, granted because of my perceived frailty, much to the chagrin of my father.

I became an altar boy there and we began to attend St. Francis Church, one of the few inland reminders of the original missionary conquests of Padre Junipero Serra along the coast. The music was better and the congregation more lively. The Church had the Franciscan effervescent aesthetic easily recognizable as distinct, say, from the more rarefied tastes of the Camaldoli, and Jesuit baroque. As in the multi-layered mother church, the Basilica of Assisi, the walls of the Franciscan churches are covered with brightly painted frescoes. In those days before the Vatican Council's radical reforms, their liturgies were more sumptuous and engaging than anyone else's. My favorite was the Easter vigil. On Good Friday, the church would be stripped of all flowers, candles, and holy water. The statues would be covered with purple cloths. Before dawn on Holy Saturday morning, we would gather in the cold outside the church where priests dressed only in white linen liturgical undergarments would ritualistically recreate the sacred elements. The new fire would be kindled from flint and charcoal to torch the Paschal Candle that symbolized the pillar of fire that led the Hebrews out of Egypt, and also Christ rising from the dead. Father John would don a heavy gold brocaded vestment, being very careful not to muss his hair, hold the phallic candle high above his head, and enter the dark church, chanting three times as he slowly made his way into the darkness, *"Lumen Christi."* At each chant, we would all fall on our knees as various groups of candles in the church would be lit until, at the third chant, the whole church was aglow. Then his golden voice would intone the ancient liturgical hymn, the *Exultet,* reciting the story of creation, the history of the Jews in Egypt and the Promised Land, and the birth of Jesus, culminating in the *Gloria in excelsis Deo,* at which point we altar boys rang hundreds of little bells, while old Brother Ludger pulled hidden drawstrings that whisked away in a flash all the purple coverings over the statues of the saints. The steeple bells would ring, and as the choir chanted the *Gloria,* a special Easter orchestra would accompany the organ with kettle drums and trumpets signaling Jesus's glorious emergence from his tomb, the sign that our own eternal salvation (or damnation) would be a very bodily event, not just the bliss (or agony) of an etheric soul.

When I entered the back sacristy reserved for altar boys early in the morning, I felt like Dorothy blown into Oz as my shirt and corduroys disappeared under a wool cassock, red or black depending on the ritual season, topped by a white surplice either delicate lace or plain linen depending on the solemnity of the occasion. As I worked my way into seniority, I got more exotic assignments. On occasions like Christmas, I sometimes was assigned to wield the incenser, a golden bucket on the end of a long chain holding glowing charcoal for grains of frankincense. At intervals during the mass, I would approach the priests, giving each a specified number of swings depending on their rank. Then I would swing the long chain at my fellow altar boys and finally at the congregation out beyond the communion rail. At festivals like *Corpus Christi* or May Day, I sometimes got to carry the processional cross, leading the long line of priests and altar boys and the crowned little girl representing the Virgin through the Church aisles out onto the sidewalk across from Sutter's Fort.

My favorite ritual was the dousing of people with holy water. I would hold the silver bucket filled with water while the priest carried an elaborately wrought silver scepter encrusted with jewels. Walking very rapidly throughout the aisles, he would dip the scepter in my bucket, and then wave it vigorously over the people, splashing water everywhere, while chanting the ancient psalm *"Asperges me"* ("Wash me, O Lord, with hyssop and I shall be made whiter than snow"). Loneliness, illness, small-mindedness floated away with the incense, leaving me in the psychedelic space of the sanctuary covered with bright murals of Yahweh creating Adam and Eve, Abraham meeting Melchisedech at the gates of proto-Jerusalem, Jesus rising from the dead into glory followed by his mother.

However, the price for those inspiring flights of fancy out of day-to-day bleakness was a rapidly growing sense of guilt backed up with fears of Hell. At the same time that I was discovering Franciscan ritual, I was experiencing the first ecstasies of erections and orgasm, pleasures far beyond the pale of anything I had imagined, so intense that they were worth sacrificing eternal bliss, but in fear and trembling. I was masturbating so much in those days, both by myself and with neighborhood boys, that I couldn't even begin to count, the number being so great that I was ashamed to tell the priest in confession.

It is hard, I think, for non-Catholics, and even perhaps modern Catholics, to grasp the terror of the ordinary moral teaching of that era. The stakes were unimaginably high. Hell, like Heaven, was a physical place not unlike Earth. Our entire being, body and soul, would exist forever in one place or another. Hell was always much easier for me to imagine than Heaven, because I had many analogues for it in pain and fear, while I had few experiences of bliss to extrapolate for Heaven. Hell was an actual physical place where the sinner in his or her actual fleshy body would endure real burning forever. Because of its eternal irrevocable severity, it was attainable only through a major and consciously deliberate decision to violate the heart of one of God's commandments. Lesser violations—cheating on tests, stealing a few things from the supermarket, lying to one's parents—were worthy of varying degrees of descent into the ephemeral pits of Purgatory. The only commandment that admitted of no degrees was the Sixth, forbidding the least deliberate sexual pleasure except for the unavoidable accidental pleasure derived from unprovoked "nocturnal emissions," or from a properly wedded husband's inserting his penis into his wife's vagina for the sake of having yet another child to increase the size of the Body of Christ. Taking pleasure in soaping one's genitals in the bath, looking sensually at them in the mirror, or at another boy's in the showers after gym class, letting oneself get "aroused" dancing too close to one's partner at the weekly Catholic Youth Organization dance—any such activity was worthy in itself of eternal damnation. This is not an exaggeration. Every religious teacher I knew well into Jesuit theology affirmed this moral policy.

Non-Catholics often romanticize the Catholic confession as an easy comfort, assuming that it promotes honesty and direct expression of hidden affairs of the soul followed by relief of guilt. For me, it was just the opposite, because each of my confessions increased my stock of unforgiven sins. For any sins to be absolved, you had to be sorry for having committed them. The Baltimore Catechism defined two sorts of sorrow:

1. perfect contrition which occurred when you were sorry for doing the acts, not because you feared Hell but only because you loved God so much you regretted offending Him; and

2. imperfect contrition, when you were sorry because you didn't want to burn in Hell or Purgatory.

In the second case, the only way to be forgiven was by confessing every single sin to the priest in confession. If you withheld any single one, or failed to give its specific category, the confession was not only invalid, but it increased the amount of sinfulness asymptotically; one would have to add that plus the invalidly confessed previous sins to future confessions. Because I was at least sane enough not to believe that my delicious skin rubbings could cause much bother to the Creator of the vast universe, I couldn't bring myself to perfect contrition. I knew that these pleasurable interludes jeopardized my soul not because they insulted God but because they were against the law. The only way to save myself from damnation was legalistic confession.

There is a strangely dissociated aspect to the authorized practice of Catholic confession. To be forgiven, we did indeed have to confess each of our serious sins, but in a highly abstract way: "species and number" only, where species referred to the particular violated subset of one of the Ten Commandments or six commandments of the Church. At my frequent confessions, instead of saying that I jacked off with my buddies every chance we got this week, in my neighbor's toolshed, putting our hands in each other's pants, often taking our clothes off and rubbing up against each other, finding our fathers' old *Esquire* magazines and holding up their sexy pictures by the famous soft pornographic illustrator Varga for our buddies to jack off with, playing strip poker slavering with desire until we finally got all our clothes off in an orgy of rubbing and handling (some hinted at sucking, but we never dared to venture that far!)—instead of all that, I would say in barely audible whispers in the dark confessional box to a priest: "I violated the Sixth Commandment about ten times ["number"]."

"With yourself or another ["species"]?" would come from behind the shadowy grate.

"Oh, just with myself, Father," I would reply, justifying the lie to myself, as would Bill Clinton many decades later, with the thought that "with another" meant inserting your penis into a girl's vagina. To admit doing it with other boys would admit to early warnings of dreaded homosexuality.

Years of talking that way week after week in such a sacred precinct, putting a great deal of creative effort into finding the phrases that would mask, even to myself, the diabolical evils I was practicing, got into my bones, leading me to think more and more abstractly about what was actually happening. In contrast to what non-Catholics often imagine to be a dishonest relief afforded by the easy confession of sins, I kept feeling increasingly guilty, knowing that each orgasm brought me closer to eternal damnation and I was not being forgiven because I wasn't telling the full number and species of my sins. The confessional became a musty and stifling cave of shame, covered with heavy velvet drapes to muffle the sounds, with the priest hidden behind a screen in the dark. Despite the whispers and the dim light, I always feared he could make out my familiar voice, or worse, that when he had entered or left the box, he noticed me kneeling in the pews outside. Faced with this humiliating situation, I had to find strategies to avoid telling the whole story. In doing so, I fell deeper into a bleak sense of hopelessness, feeling powerless to stop pursuing these juicy delights, and therefore fated towards damnation.

This abstract system for sin-accounting has something to do with the pedophilia crisis in the Church. In addition to the sexually repressive canons of celibacy, the confessional accounting methods make it easy for priests to overlook the traumatic effects of their transgressions. Just as I learned to gloss over the thousands of sexual sins of many species under the single rubric "self-abuse with myself alone," so the bishops and priests involved in countless scandals could easily think of fleeting encounters in dormitories and seminaries as harmless touchings in the dark, not demanding careful scrutiny as to the intricate embodied details of what actually happens to the vulnerable young recipients of these poignant touches.

Catholicism long held the center of my attentions precisely because of its contrasts between a transcendent surreality and the repulsive repressiveness of my pubescent sexuality, far more intriguing to me than what I considered to be a banal human-scale Protestant Christianity. Swishing around on the altar at funerals

with the priests in their heavy black brocades chanting the *Dies
Irae,* and processing in glittery white on the feast of Corpus Christi
to the *Pange Lingua Gloriosi* gave me a sense of a magic world more
intriguing than real estate, banking, and heavy construction. But
underneath my cassock, the ebbs and flows of my newly awakened
penis seemed like a Boschean demon luring me towards the secret-
ly attractive fires of damnation. I was terrified to be out of control
of my eternal destiny, but at the same time, I had to stay mentally
alert to figure out these high-stakes puzzles.

Those fantasy-like rituals set the stage for what has been a life-
long inquiry into the complexities of the body. On the one hand,
the processions, elaborate gestures, Gregorian chant, and ancient
choreographies hinted at a spirituality that was full-bodied in contrast to the ethereal feel of the Cathedral liturgies. At the same time,
my throbbing pubescent sins clouded my pleasure in those rituals.
With hundreds of people watching me, I felt I had to take Holy
Communion or be judged as hiding serious sins unable to be confessed. Yet each sinful communion kept adding to my eternal debt.
My body was Armageddon where the armies of Jesus and Satan
did battle for my soul, just as described by St. Ignatius of Loyola in
his *Spiritual Exercises.*

It was only late in life that I came to realize that I had been raised
in an idiosyncratic version of Christianity peculiar to Ireland and a
few other localities. In the fall of 1993, I was in the eleventh-century
Camaldoli Monastery in the Apennines above Arezzo in Italy with
twenty-five others including Catholic monks, Jewish artists, a Native
American medicine man, a Cairo Muslim, orthodox monks from
Russia, and a number of teachers of different body practices. We
were there as part of a long-term project in which I gathered together groups of bodyworkers and religious leaders from different

traditions with the hope that if religious people would focus more on their commonalities in healing, ritual, and nonverbal aspects of spirituality rather than abstract dogma, they might more fruitfully collaborate in dealing with some of the daunting challenges facing the world today.

On this particular morning, Vincent and Rosemarie Harding were conducting the session in the room where Lorenzo de Medici launched the *Accademia,* the gathering of artists and philosophers who would shape the Florentine Renaissance. The Hardings have been leaders in the Freedom Movement since its beginnings, close associates of Martin Luther King, Jr., Dr. Howard Thurman, and many others. Vincent is a historian of the crossings from Africa. Rosemarie, until her death, was a gifted healer, social worker, and teacher. They had arranged a presentation of the version of body and spirit emerging from the slave tradition—part lecture about the function of the Christian churches in nurturing the spirit of African Americans in their long journeys to civil rights; part privately made recordings. They spoke of John Coltrane, Duke Ellington, Don Shirley, and many others. Fanny Lou Hamer, though, was the center of the session. Vincent described her as rising from being a sharecropper "absolutely extraneous to anything that was important" to becoming one of the greatest prophets of the Movement. After attending one of Vincent's workshops in Mississippi, where he had encouraged people to put their beliefs into practice, she sat on the White side of a local bus station, was put in prison, and severely beaten, after which she began to grow into her eventual position of leadership within the community. Vincent played his own tape of her singing Christian songs that she rewrote for the Movement, like "Go Tell It on the Mountain." Originally a Christmas song popular among the slaves, she changed its climactic stanza from "Jesus Christ has come" to "Let my people go." He used her rewritten songs to show how the community transformed their familiar Christian music and prayers to fuel the courage and passion required for gaining freedom.

The Hardings also played little-known speeches of Martin Luther King, Jr., whose words, like Fanny Lou Hamer's, were based on the Gospels reworded for the freedom struggles. The Hardings spoke of how for them the church was where the Freedom Movement was born; it was the one place where the slave owners did not exercise absolute domination. They were able to preserve their sacred music and dances by embedding them within the Christian rites.

As they spoke and played these recordings, I wondered why Christianity had been so different for me, my mother, and all our Irish Catholic relatives: joyless, rigid, eviscerating, generating extreme dependency on the authority of others such as doctors, teachers, and the Pope. In that moment, with the bright fall light penetrating the lead-paned windows looking far out over the Umbrian forests, I realized that I had not been raised simply as a Christian, or a Roman Catholic, but as an Irish Catholic whose lineage went back to Maynooth Seminary outside Dublin, where most of the Sacramento priests had been trained.

Maynooth occupied a unique place in the international Catholic community as the last bastion of a strange little Catholic sect that originated with a Belgian theologian named Jansenius in the nineteenth century and flourished for a time in the French monastery of *Port Royal des Champs*. It was a Catholic version of Calvinist terror: God the Father is a God of vengeance, impossible to approach in his overweaning majesty. Jesus alone can bridge the gap, but he would only mediate for the rare person who was utterly pure, devoid of the slightest turn towards the sensual pleasures of food, music, art, and especially sex. In this view, only the smallest percentage of believers would be saved; the rest, lost to eternal damnation.

As you might guess, this ascetic theology did not find a ready audience among the sensual French, with the exception of a few dour intellectuals like Pascal. But the Irish, with their dank spirits and ancient history of self-inflicted violence, took to Jansenism right away. Its fertile vigor lost at Port Royal, the movement found more hospitable soil at Maynooth, where armies of missionaries continue to be trained to carry this dark spirituality to the United States, Canada, Australia, and even the heart of Africa, where one of my grandfather Joe's cousins created such a devoted following as a White Father and bishop in Zambia that he is now in the process of being canonized a saint. Like the illusions of Sodom and Gomorrah, however, it turned out that many of the priests and bishops who graduated from Maynooth were engaging in out-of-control lascivious desires for young boys and married women under the guise of moral severity, with the result that the Jansenist hold over Southern Ireland has rapidly weakened.

It was only here at Camaldoli, in the presence of this heart-wrenching drama recounted by the Hardings, that I realized that I had been schooled in that marginal Jansenist version of Catholicism, focused not on joyful redemption and mystical union with the divine and compassion for weak human beings based on that ecstasy, but on a slavish adherence to moral prescriptions about private behavior. No wonder I had spent most of my adulthood engaged in the practice and study of bodywork and the meaning of the human body, the sacrament of the soul's meeting with Jesus.

Even in the 1960s Church, revitalized by Pope John XXIII, the Council, and the various sociopolitical movements housed within the churches, the voices were still pale imitations of Joan Baez and Bob Dylan, and the new "liturgical dance" was formal and aestheticized. Vatican II's reintroduction of the ancient rituals of the holding of hands during the Our Father and the "kiss of peace" just before the distribution of Holy Communion revealed the deep longing for engaging the full body in the liturgy. Suddenly there were a few moments of never-before-seen vitality among the congregation—smiles, excitement, warmth, movement. Even now, it is one of the few passing moments during the hour in which most everyone seems truly alive, although the atmosphere is still a long way from the boisterous sound and vital movements of the African American churches with their charismatic preachers crying "Freedom! Courage!"

Conservatives made an enormous outcry about these timid gestures, out of all proportion to their simplicity, and contrary to the fact that the practice was well grounded in the history of the earliest liturgies in the Roman Catacombs. They crankily complained that these simple contacts with one's neighbors in the pews, along with replacing arcane Latin with the common language, undermined the very essence of polite Latin ritual and theology. And, in some ways, they were right; it was indeed a sign of a different kind of spirituality, one that is older, more communal, less priest- and pope-centered, pushing us closer to some of our Protestant neighbors who were not quite so dour about sex, and more democratic.

How is it that these branches of Christianity, sharing the same sources of moral authority in the Bible and early Church history, could differ so drastically about such fundamental realities as the body and sexuality? There are many factors at play. The primal origins of Christianity among the Jewish community in Palestine were transformed by each country and region in which they took new root: Syria, Greece, Rome, Russia, Spain, Ireland, the Mediterranean, Africa, and eventually Central Africa after the slave trade had begun. In the third century, poorly educated missionary monks with dark anti-sensual attitudes were sent out by the Pope to translate Jesus's peasant teachings to convert the barbaric Celts. Long before it ever reached Boston and Sacramento, Catholicism had become a state religion and developed the austerities embodied by Maynooth. The Jesuit Catholicism that shaped my young adult life turned out to be similarly localized. Its origins were in fourth-century Spain, where Rome had sent similar groups of monks to evangelize the Visigoths. It was not until a thousand years later, at the peak of the Inquisition when Catholicism was a state Church with enormous secular power, that Ignatius wrote his rule for Jesuit religious life. By dramatic contrast, African-American Christian churches were created in the New World when European missionaries evangelized the slaves who were already steeped in ancient African religions, which placed central emphasis on the divine as manifested in the Earth, its seasons, the body, birth, sickness, and death. Millennia before northern Christian and Islamic missionaries ventured into the Congo or the Gold Coast, the myriad tribes had developed ancient liturgies to ritualize their vision in the dance, chant, and music that have shaped the American aesthetic. Unlike the Irish, Africans were brought here by force, and then evangelized. My Church was Irish and Spanish, as well as Catholic. The Hardings' was more African than American.

And yet, there was a core that united all of us at Camaldoli, hard to express. Judaism, Christianity, and Islam are historical religions whose theologies have been shaped by longings for a just society forged out of long histories of weathering oppressive political regimes—Egyptian, Babylonian, Imperial Roman, British, American. In their religiously based fervor for human freedom and the importance of the human body and its needs, they differ from the more timeless apolitical traditions of Hinduism and Gnosticism. That fervor continues to roil about in my own soul, prompting me to keep looking beyond the close-to-hand, and to purge the overlays of moral superiority and isolation from that ancient humanism.

✧

Only late in life did I learn from Native American, Asian, and African-American friends a radically different attitude towards family, based on a spirituality that placed family and ancestors at the center of ethical behavior.

In the 1980s I had as a student a Vietnamese Buddhist philosopher, who now works as a counselor for fellow refugees in the Bay
Area. He once described a particular ceremony that marked the
Vietnamese New Year in which the family gathered to clean the
tombs of the ancestors. This specific occasion was during the war.
One of his uncles was Viet Minh; another, Viet Cong. Knowing that
they would be executed as collaborators with the enemy if anyone
saw them together, they risked their lives to return for that ceremony. He wrote in an essay for my class: "In Vietnam the body of the
dead not only makes the soil become holy but also makes life itself
become more meaningful. So they would rather die meaningfully
than live meaninglessly."

Here was exactly the opposite of my spiritual upbringing. I read-
ily gave up my family to seek a more interesting life on my own,
untethered from earthly connections. By stark contrast, these men,
conscripted by ideologies spawned in Europe and wreaking violence upon ancient Asia, were willing to give up their lives to honor
their family and the soil sanctified by their remains.

The photo of Aunt Charlotte's wedding and the story of the
Vietnamese grave cleansing are markers to me of a different way to
motivate our lives—less earth-shattering, closer to home and modest. I think of this story now when I go with my mother and son on
Christmas and Easter to clean my father's grave and help my mother decorate it with a small Christmas tree or an Easter bouquet.

7

Forbidden Books

FROM THE ORIGINS OF POPULAR READING IN THE 1400S with Gutenberg's publication of the Bible in vernacular German up until now, defenders of the missionary position have feared books, not without reason. Certain kinds of books, including the Bible itself, undermine missionary convictions, creating in the reading believer a dangerous sense of ambiguity as he or she confronts the intricacies of human subjectivity and the infinitely wide range of thoughtful and moral approaches to the ultimate meanings of life.

Just before the Velvet Revolution in Prague, I recall reading, with the shock of recognition of its rightness, a sentence of Vaclav Havel in which he said that the first act of a totalitarian regime is to destroy grammar. Bureaucratized vocabularies, devoid of allusion and metaphor, are so removed from fleshy lives that they make it possible to carry on the most atrocious events—genocides, indiscriminate bombing and land-mining, devastations of the natural environment—as if they were simply rational ways for carrying on political life, like new procedures for accounting. In the face of such dissociated language, sensible ordinary people are left mute to defend their versions of the world. Constant efforts have been made by institutions to inhibit access to books and to eviscerate ancient, intricate, raw vernaculars; these efforts range from the Roman Inquisition to the Hitler, Stalinist, and Maoist terrors of the last century, to the current efforts by mullahs and Christian ministers to restrict access to books that they deem a threat to faith. The chronic violence against books extends to a harassing of their authors beyond comprehension. The meekest of men and women, solitary in their studies as they craft their texts, have been the targets of the most vicious attacks for simply writing about things as they see it.

During the vibrant days of perestroika, I was in a small group hosting the visit to San Francisco by the editor of *Pravda*, who was a boyhood friend of Gorbachev. In our discussion, I asked him how it happened that he and his friends had taken this turn away from the established order. He told of how as young teenagers, a group of them had smuggled the forbidden novels of Dostoevsky into dark cellars, where they would read and discuss them. The thick layers of narrative awakened their dormant resistance to the simplistic dogmatisms of the Kremlin and set them on their revolutionary path. His experience was parallel to my own during the Jesuit years when a handful of us surreptitiously engaged in a wide range of readings of cutting-edge writers and philosophers: Nabokov, Pynchon, Philip Roth, Wittgenstein, Heidegger, Teilhard de Chardin, and many others.

Although I am the creator of a hybrid graduate studies curriculum of philosophy, body practices, and psychology—subjects that I have studied and taught for four decades—writing has always been at the heart of that activity. Every day I see students' joy as they are able to free themselves from debilitating academic expectations to get simple sentences on the page detailing their sufferings, experiences of vitality, their peculiar perceptions of the world, their forgotten cultural heritages, and their dreams—finding out, some for the first time, that they are truly intelligent, with ancient resources in their ancestors and the Earth, dreams and insights that must be heard.

I first became aware of the revolutionary capacities of reading and writing from my childhood companion Joan Didion.

The earliest photos of me in my mother's garage were taken when I was a few months old playing on the white-sand beach at

Carmel with baby Joan. My parents and hers—Frank and Eduene—had rented a house near Charlie Chaplin's secluded retreat on the dunes bordering the Pebble Beach Golf Course. I look like any ordinary infant enjoying innocent delights of scattering sand and splashing water, while Joan, even then, has that familiar look you can see on her book jackets—a gaze that gives the impression that she peers too deeply beneath the masks of the world to be happy; bleak, without childish innocence, susceptible to seeing horrors so intense that she has to wear large sunglasses to keep them at bay, yet longing for it to be otherwise. Outside her warm presence, it is hard to locate that longing in her writing. It breaks through only in a few passages, like the desperate final sentence of *The Last Thing He Wanted*. Even though she has just written the termination of the late-blooming romance between Elena McMahon and Treat Morrison by having him assassinated as they are finally on their way to fall into each other's arms, she laments: "I want those two to have been together all their lives." Or in *Where I Was From*, where she writes of walking along the river's edge in Sacramento's theme park "Old Town" with her mother and daughter Quintana, awash in nostalgic fantasies of her pioneering roots. It suddenly occurs to her that Quintana is an adopted child, not of these roots. The nostalgic illusions of biological history fall away in her realization that "It was only Quintana who was real." And now, tragically, Quintana too is gone, long before her time.

In *Slouching Towards Bethlehem*, Joan writes about my fourth birthday party, of which there is also a photo in my mother's garage: I stand in my white collared shirt, an angelic smile covering my already vindictive anger; big cousin Gordon, now dead of prostate cancer, looms over me at my right, oblivious of the darkness that surrounds us; Joan like a barn owl at my left, next to sweet-looking Sally Fletcher, daughter of our pharmacist, and wide-eyed Sue Mayhood, whose father Jack owned the first stylish men's store in town.

When Joan started junior high school, her mother Eduene told my mother with some distress that Joan's seventh-grade essay had been one of two read at the Thanksgiving PTA meeting as examples of outstanding quality: one was by a boy on how much we all have to be thankful for, living in this fertile valley. Hers was on the hypocrisy of Thanksgiving when we neglect to acknowledge the pernicious sources of our prosperity. Even though I never got to read that essay, Eduene's mention of it seemed almost as exciting as ferreting out erotic passages from my father's paperbacks. One rarely questioned the surface pretensions that we were all so happy on our holidays when my father and uncles were getting drunker and meaner by the minute with the women acting cheery, while I just sat watching in a depressed torpor. That she dared to go so far as to write a public essay addressing that smog of denial was a juicy surge out of the stagnant currents of our life. It was a first hint that writing could be a revolutionary act, more radical than fleeing Sacramento, divorcing one's spouse, or taking to the streets in protest. To this day, I have that same feeling when I read her newest essay in the *New York Review of Books* skewering the latest deceptions of Washington policy, unmasking the growing lust for power that motivates our public servants, or her sentimentality-free account of her grief in the face of the death of her loved ones.

✧

As with Joan, reading and writing have marked my path out of a certain childhood torpor. Many people find the world outside the narrow confines of their neighborhoods by getting out and experiencing it—traveling, talking with strangers, playing sports, trading, and making love to people very different from themselves. My Aunt Charlotte's late husband Bill was for me an example of those venturesome people. When he was sixteen and fed up with his abusive father, he mounted an eastbound train from his hometown in Minnesota and never went back.

Books were my train out of town. I began to mount their silent cars for distant journeys as far back as I can remember, using my childhood asthma as an excuse to spend my days in our well-insulated house on N Street, as hermetic as Marcel Proust's cork-lined room on *rue Hamelin*. My father read to me after Dr. Lorenz put me in the hospital when I was four years old, fearing that I might have spinal meningitis. He continued to read to me when I was confined to my bed for weeks each spring with bronchitis: the complete Oz series, the Arabian Nights, Hans Brinker and the Silver Skates, Black Beauty, Huck Finn, and Tom Sawyer.

The old city of Sacramento exuded a seductive air of peace and containment with its elm-lined geometric streets laid out like the imperial grid in Kyoto. The adults among whom we grew up were so relieved to have at long last moved out of the poverty of their parents, just barely having survived the Great Depression, that they could not bring themselves to care about the Mexican and Dust Bowl families struggling in their hovels along the river, fueling the farm and construction economies with their back-breaking labor. One of my best friends as a child was an African-American neighbor, at a time when there were only a few in Sacramento, before the World War II Vallejo shipyards and the Valley Air Force bases drew a large population of workers from places like St. Louis, Chicago, and the deep South. I knew nothing at all about his family. I winced and angrily complained when my parents' friends would make mean remarks about Blacks, not understanding how skin color could preempt neighborliness. It would be many years, no thanks to my early schooling, before I had any sense of African-American history. I can recall reading only brief paragraphs about slavery; I entered adulthood under the impression that Abraham Lincoln had ended it once and for all, and it was only innate laziness born of being raised in tropical climates that made it difficult for African-Americans moving into Southside Park and Oak Park after the war to break out of their poverty. To this day, my mother still recalls when my college friend and former State legislator John Vasconcellos brought his African-American assistant over for a party. It was the only time in her nearly a century of living there that a person of color entered her home.

The schools reflected that head-in-the-sand mentality of old Sacramento. Not in public grade schools, high school, or college did I learn about the prices paid to establish our seemingly tranquil Valley. We were saturated with the mythologies that gave birth to Hollywood Westerns: John Sutter and the Donner Party, Kit Carson, Admiral Vallejo, and John Fremont—heroes making the way for our ancestors to find a better life in a vast uninhabited New World. I don't remember a single word about the slaughter of the Maidu, the Wintu, and the Yana right here on these very fields where we now lived. We learned only the cleansed reports of the happy discoveries of gold in the foothills, pictured as an Eden where no one had lived before, and of Junipero Serra's saintly campaigns up the coast bringing Christian joy to the many tribes—Chumash, Salinans, Esselens, Tipai—who, it was said, had been living in pagan squalor and ignorance. I knew nothing about the dark politics of Church and State through the ages. The Mayflower, the Conquistadors, Pericles, the *Pax Romana,* Lewis and Clark, and the Louisiana and Gadsden Purchases were the chapter headings. Zapata, Sitting Bull, Tojo, and Hitler played the bad guys for the simple dramas made of history—that era's version of Fidel Castro, Osama bin Laden, and Saddam Hussein. Catechism class was only about Jesus and the history of the Popes, with fleeting reference to Luther and Calvin as dour renegades who drank a lot and told scatological stories, and brief dismissals of the horrors of the Roman and Spanish Inquisitions as revisions of history constructed by Jews and Protestants (like Great-Grandmother Lucy) to discredit our infallible Church.

Scattered about our neighborhoods were many vital spiritual traditions about which I knew nothing but the grossest stereotypes picked up over dinner table conversation. The oldest church in Sacramento is a Japanese Buddhist Church a few blocks from our house. A Jewish synagogue was built soon after. I have vivid memories of the celebrations of Chinese New Year downtown near the Union Pacific Railway Station: dragons and firecrackers, chow mein and won ton soup. I knew that my relatives always turned to Chinese physicians when their own doctors failed, finding remarkable success with herbs and needles. Although a Chinese family owned the market at the corner of our block, and the laundry down the street, and we often went to Frank Fat's restaurant, I never thought about what their lives might be like until I read Maxine Hong Kingston's *Woman Warrior,* which describes her Chinese community just down Highway 99 in Stockton. Every summer on our drive to a long vacation by the Monterey Bay, we would stop for an iced lemon Coke in the drugstore next door to the hellish laundry where her family was virtually incarcerated, struggling to eke out a living. Not until I was far into adulthood, with decades of advanced education behind me, would I learn that these fleeting figures, whom I hardly noticed and had been taught to think of as somewhat pathetic and primitive, were in fact bearers of bodies of knowledge, healing, and art that far surpassed the crude traditions of our families. I grew up with not the slightest idea about these ancient wisdom traditions, except that their beliefs were misguided, not up to our standards of an advanced Christian civilization. Steeped in such ignorance, it was not hard for our Euro-American families to support the incarceration of the Japanese-Americans during the war, even though most of their forebears had settled in Sacramento before our own.

There was virtually no mention of the Old Worlds from which our families had come. My Irish cousins never spoke of the tortured history of Ireland, about which I knew virtually nothing until my forties, when I began to read Irish novels in preparation for my first visit there—Edna O'Brien, Patrick McCourt, Roddy Doyle, John McGahern. Late in their life, my mother and father made their first visit there. Despite the fact that the tiny village of Kilbeggan, where my mother's father was born, is less than two hours' drive from Dublin, my mother said it was too much trouble to go there. I finally made that journey in 1980, and within fifteen minutes of walking into the lone grocery store and introducing myself, many cousins living on farms nearby started showing up and bringing me into their homes. The next day I found Joe Hanlon's birth records in the parish church. Over rashers of bacon and too much of their home-brewed poteen, I learned of the hard history of the family, the potato famine of the 1800s, the constant displacement of the Irish by the British landowners, the destruction of the Irish language by the enforced teaching of English in the schools, the British nurturing of the conflicts between the Presbyterian northerners imported from Scotland to Belfast, and the Roman Catholic southerners. I got a sense that the history of brutal displacement and betrayals accounted in part for the chronic depression of Grandpa Joe and his relatives over on 24th Street.

I was standing on a street corner one day in Dublin waiting for the bus to arrive. A tall thin well-contained man in his sixties wearing a gray suit, vest, and tie was waiting next to me. As we chatted, I began to edge into the subject of how he came to be in Dublin. His face slowly turned crimson as he told of how he had been born and raised and married in Belfast and how in the middle of the night a few days after the birth of their first daughter, the British soldiers had come and expelled them from their home. "Let the IRA blow them up," he said. I grew so angry as I learned more details of this tragic history that I remember standing in Westminster Cathedral in London on my way back to Paris wanting to blow up the whole thing, just like a young IRA thug. That anger is so deep in my family bones that I still feel that way when I enter San Francisco's Grace Cathedral, despite my more rational understanding of the complexities of history.

My father's parents had come from Sweden and Norway at the turn of the century. I grew up not knowing a single thing about the history or cultures of Scandinavia save for a few foods like my Grandmother Matilda's tiny Swedish meatballs, and my Grandfather Jul's pickled pigs' feet. Jul would get very angry if my grandmother ever used Swedish phrases: "We are Americans," he would assert. We have not the slightest clue about how my great-grandmother's family made their way as far as Roodhouse, a little town in central Illinois, in the mid-1800s where they settled before they took the railroad to Sacramento. My mother and her cousins say it never occurred to them to ask.

Even though I was more confined than most because of my sicknesses, the narrowness of my life was not particularly unusual. Sacramento was a claustrophobic space capsule, a Leibnizian windowless monad floating in the vastness of the Valley: only what we could see close up was worth thinking about. Best forget about the rest outside our ken.

I never saw books in the houses of either of my grandparents. My mother and father must have been the first in their families to take up regular reading. Even though my father worked six and sometimes seven days a week on heavy construction, he was always reading pulp fiction, mostly thrillers and detective stories. When I approached adolescence, I stole frequent looks at his Mickey Spillane books to find isolated paragraphs where the tough good-guy detective would take a few moments away from his tracking a killer to strip the bra and panties off a girl standing next to him in the elevator to feel her up and pull off a quick fuck.

My mother has been a reader as long as I can remember. Even though she, like my father, did not have more than a high-school *education,* she always seemed interested in books. She joined a literary book-of-the-month club when I was a boy. Of the many titles that would arrive, I remember only *Van Loon's Lives,* a very big book which sat on her nightstand for a long time. Until her mid-nineties, when macular degeneration set in, she read every day, mostly historical and romance novels, but often a biography or a history book. Strangely, she had little to say about them. For instance, she finished Barbara Kingsolver's epic, *The Poisonwood Bible,* a great achievement for a woman of my mother's age with cataracts. The book is intense in its condemnation of the severe pains visited upon women and children by dissociated husbands, American colonialists, and Christian missionaries, all sensitive topics for her. I imagine that she had many intricate, even conflicting thoughts reading it, but when I made attempts to discuss it with her, curious about how she might deal now in her later years with all those delicate topics, hoping for some wise words to help me on my own way, she just spoke about how long it was, with some pride that she had finished it.

Another clue I have that reading occupied an important place in the secret inner lives of my parents is that when television finally arrived in our home, late in their lives, they still continued to read every day. They would watch a couple of hours of television, turn it off, and sit quietly reading before going to bed. To this day, my mother confines herself to a meagre five channels through her antenna. When I offer to have cable installed, she refuses, saying she does not want television to become so attractive that she will become immersed in it.

The constant example of their own reading and their daily reading to me as a child set the stage for my absorption in books. Debilitation by asthma and feelings of isolation as an only child propelled me headlong into many more different kinds of reading than my parents and my childhood buddies would ever undertake.

I was carried forward by the intuition that books were leading me out of the constrictions I felt, not just in my lungs, but in my limbs, my imagination, my thinking, my sexuality, my relations with other people.

Brother Philip became my first real guide into the spacious hopes associated with this bookish world when I began Christian Brothers High School, out on Broadway near the Tower Theatre. My mother's father Joe Hanlon had graduated from Christian Brothers in 1896 when it was downtown, across from the Cathedral of the Blessed Sacrament. It was razed to make way for Weinstock and Lubin's Department Store in 1923, the year before my father would enroll at their new Broadway campus, from which he graduated in 1927. There are conflicting stories about why his nominally Lutheran parents chose to remove him from the public Sacramento High School after his freshman year and send him to a private Catholic school. My mother says it was because all his friends were there. My aunts Charlotte and Gladys say it was because he wanted to play football. He used to brag that it was because he was a discipline problem and the Brothers were known for not sparing the rod. At a recent reunion, one of my classmates gave a toast in which he joked that what we thought of as a private school was actually a reformatory.

The aristocratic Brother Benignus had founded "The Brothers of the Christian Schools" in 1650 in Paris for poor street urchins who, it was thought, often needed a beating to teach them obedience. Until the post-war era when such measures came to be outlawed in America, boys were routinely struck by the Brothers when they got out of line. Many stories were passed down, no doubt embellished, about instances of the Brothers' violence. Old Brother Conrad, in his seventies when I was a student there, would occasionally substitute when one of our other teachers was absent. He seemed as if he were summoning up all his energies to keep himself from using his pointer to smash the fingers of one or another of us told to sit quietly with our hands flat out on our desks as he drilled us in algebra. We all had heard our fathers talking about how he would pick them up and whack their heads against the wall when they got feisty or spoke out of turn. Our Latin teacher, Monsignor O'Connor, an Irish missionary from Maynooth Seminary—looking like something out of Fritz Murnau's *Nosferatu,* short and plump, porcelain flesh, beady eyes, long pointed nose—dressed in black robes with the monsignorial purple buttons and sash, and always carried a rod. Now, with the new laws protecting students from abuse, he had to restrict himself to whacking it hard on the desk to demand quiet. With a grin showing his yellow teeth, he would come up behind us in the yard and pinch us very hard. His strange demeanor and his quirky guidance through Julius Caesar's *Gallic Wars* made me so interested in Latin literature that I, and only two others, opted to study it for all four years of high school, eventually learning to speak and write it.

Despite this atmosphere of old European Christian sado-masochism, I found an excitement in this exclusive world of men with egg-stained soutanes and days-old stubble, impolitely getting riled, scratching their balls, having a good time playing with us on the schoolyard. I was relieved to be liberated from the exclusive control of well-groomed women teachers who quietly demanded genteel behavior while they polished their nails. Learning here was fleshy, related to some kind of spiritual vision beyond just preparing to be a good working citizen.

The wild passionate Brother Philip, who looked and behaved like James Dean, was my teacher in mathematics, science, and religion every one of the four years. He saw beyond my seeming mediocre intellectual talents and fear into a heretofore undeveloped bright and yearning enthusiasm. He was a young, feisty, ex-bantam-weight State boxing champion from the Oakland slums, angry about the miseries of the world, passionate about waking us up from our Valley torpor. With me, at least, he succeeded. He steered me into a very peculiar kind of reading that dealt with a high-altitude kind of thinking that I had never known before, both dizzying in its remoteness from the concreteness of everyday life and awesome in its vast perspective.

I remember clearly the very first book he gave me, Frank Sheed's *On the Trinity,* which stands out even now for its exaggerated abstraction. I still find it strange that I was so taken by it—only due, I think, to the fact that Brother Philip had given it to me, recognizing, as had no one else, that I had the rococo intelligence required to deal with it. Its elegant architectonic of medieval analysis fascinated me as much as Oz and Treasure Island once did. Sheed, who founded a Catholic publishing house in New York, crafted a layman's summary of the long medieval tradition of monks and philosophers trying to make sense of how Catholics could be considered monotheists if we worshipped Father, Son, and Holy Ghost, each of whom was declared by the Fathers of the Church to be a Person in his or its or her own right. (St. Bernard of Clairvaux had gone so far as to suggest adding Mary, making God into a Quadrinity, a view held by our Jesuit Master of Novices.)

Scholastic theologians turned to the opening sentence of John's Gospel for their central metaphor: "In the beginning was the Word, and the Word was with God, and the Word was God." They interpreted the meaning of those biblical words in light of the classic texts of Plato and Aristotle about the nature of the human mind, arguing that the inner life and structure of the Holy Trinity was like intellectual activity in which there is a knower, the act of knowing, and the expression of that knowing in language. Both Monotheism and Trinitarianism are saved by having only One Being with three substantive aspects: God the Father, knower; Jesus, the Word expressed by the Father; and the Holy Spirit, the reflective process.

Crafting sentences that would accurately express the reasonableness of believing in One God and Three Divine Persons was not a disembodied activity, attended to only by a few cloistered celibate scribes in their scriptoria. The urge to find a viable definition had found its way so deeply into the passions of believers that proper wording was the occasion for religious wars, torture, slaughter, and excommunications during the first Christian millennium.

While my contemporaries were outside playing sandlot baseball and basketball, I sat by the hour in our quiet living room pouring over this and similar abstract books by Catholic intellectuals like Gilbert Keith Chesterton and John Henry Newman. For me they were like brilliantly designed topographical maps of a magic land far away, where unimaginably varied choirs of angels and armies of devils battled for our souls with powers as glamorous as those of the Jedi Knights, Lord Voldemort, and Darth Vader. Giving myself over to their wild flights of fantasy felt like a rush of cocaine: they gave hints of an infinitely spacious divine realm, vaster than anyone could imagine, with delights and apocalyptic dangers not capable of being corralled by human language, a land of which I had the barest hints somewhere deep in my soul, but not the slightest notion of how to get there.

Brother Philip, who set me on my lifetime journey of studying philosophy and theology, was not a scholar in those fields, but his eyes glistened when he spoke about them. He paid careful attention to me when I told him about what I was finding in the books he gave me. He was curious about me and my images of what my future life might become. Unlike most of my public school teachers, and secular teachers I would encounter later in life, he was more interested in nurturing our spirits than in making us good citizens and family men.

✦

> I mean for me the great thing about reading is it's eucharistic for me. You take somebody's words into your body, somebody else's suffering and feeling, and we're transformed by it. There's nothing that makes me feel less lonely.
>
> —MARY KARR[14]

Incorporating texts into my body also made me less lonely, living as I did among throngs of imagined friends from every age and every country, even ones who never existed. And, as with the rituals surrounding the eucharist and the rules about who was eligible to receive it, reading was situated by my religious teachers within the sacred conflicts between Christ and Satan.

The Vatican's Office of the Inquisition, which was renamed "The Holy Office" in modern times to make it seem more benign (Pope Benedict XV was its director before his coronation), has an elaborate system of determining which books may be read by Catholics. There are three formal levels of review, ranging from the local *imprimi potest* ("it may be printed"), to the official diocesan censor's *nihil obstat* ("nothing stands in the way"), to the final sanction by the bishop's *imprimatur* ("let it be printed"). A book failing these examinations was either left for the dustbin or banished to the tantalizing "Index of Forbidden Books," which proscribed any number of widely read works, for reasons of their perceived dangers to morals or to Catholic dogma: Freud, Darwin, Stendahl, Joyce. A vast network of papally sanctioned examiners even ferreted out and condemned lesser known pulp fiction like *Forever Amber* and The *Amboy Dukes,* whose names I would hear being bandied about in hushed terms by my more precocious classmates when we were just entering adolescence.

Catholic teaching conferred a magic quality on many everyday activities, which to my friends reared as Protestants or Jews were just ordinary, bordering on the banal. Things like jerking off and feeling up breasts, eating and drinking, telling fibs, going to certain films, and reading certain books were clothed in a dramatic aura of eternal significance, having the potential to earn one the unending fires of Hell or transform one's body into the blissfully immortal body of Christ. These activities, so plain in themselves, were imbued through our education with the images and events of sacred history. "Sacraments" they were called in Latin, outwardly perceptible signs of hidden mysteries. Washing the newborn baby was not just for cleanliness; it was the child's initiation into the drama of death and rebirth, Heaven and Hell, requiring a protection from the germs of Satan and all his wiles. Bread was not just for muscles and brain cells; it was the flesh of the Crucified, whose meaning was fought over to the death for centuries; whose verbal expressions called forth a millennium of linguistic philosophy and theology. The orgastic embrace of husband and wife reflected the primal insertion of the promiscuous Father God into the wet unformed chaos to bring forth the divinely beautiful cosmos with its Chosen People. It also reflected the penetration of virginal Mary by the Holy Spirit and the sensual union of Christ and His Church.

Lectio divina, "divine reading," is one of those sacred practices: a daily period of reading books that were thought to be evocative of the reader's tendencies towards sanctity: the lives of the saints, the Bible, books on meditation, devotional thoughts. Although it is not one of the official Seven Sacraments (Baptism, Confirmation, Holy Communion, etc.), it is one of the oldest and most characteristic practices of Catholic spirituality, with origins in the ancient Jewish devotion to sacred texts and their interpretations.

Jesuit initiation situated my already highly developed reading habits within a context of mystical discipline. Our schedule prescribed a period of thirty minutes a day for such reading, even in the midst of intensely active work assignments and hours of study of philosophy and theology. It was for me the most joyful interlude in the tightly scheduled monastic day—vivid, bloody passages of the Bible with Yahweh accusing the Israelites of behaving like a whore begging at the gates of a city; Jesus spitting on mud and slapping it on the eyes of a blind man; accounts of holy people like Mary of the Desert, an Alexandrian prostitute who, exhausted from trying to seduce St. Anthony with her full breasts and spread legs, went over to celibacy and monastic austerity herself; or the hapless monk Arsenius, who resisted the rule against crossing legs during *lectio divina,* and was found struck dead on a dung heap, presumably possessed by the Devil.

For Jesuits and other groups of monks and nuns, Rome proscribed long lists of books that were not on the Index, but judged dangerous nonetheless for young celibates who, as the *avant garde* of Christ's army, were prime targets for the infinitely wise strategies of Satan. One of these dangerous books was Rollo May's *Man's Search for Meaning,* a heady analysis of the relevance of Martin Heidegger's thought to psychology, which, combined with the books of Carl Rogers and Abraham Maslow, formed the theoretical foundation for the birth of the Human Potential Movement. It was the first illicit book I ever touched. You cannot imagine the excitement that ensued when Father Berman, our choir director, on the verge of running off with a pretty young soprano, snuck a copy to a handful of us young seminarians, including Brother Jerry Brown, who was convinced by its line of reasoning that his religious faith was a sham and left the seminary in favor of more secular politics.

I deliberately wrote "the first illicit book I ever *touched.*" The Catholic strategy of forbidding certain things, like the incessant warnings and metaphysically complex rationalizations against paying any attention to genitals, perversely conferred a disproportionate amount of power on the object, albeit an evil one. To open such a book was as exciting as touching one's penis. In both cases, according to Church teaching, to do so was to venture out of the prosaic world into an archaic blood-curdling battle between two infinitely strong forces representing Good and Evil, with a humanly frail Jesus charged with the task of mobilizing the world on the side of Good.

Chardin

If you are not familiar with the medieval cast of Catholic seminary life, you may be surprised to know that until Vatican II in the mid-1960s, we were forbidden to read any books written by the popular Jesuit archaeologist Pierre Teilhard de Chardin because he was rightly perceived by the Vatican as a serious challenger to the traditional Roman Catholic condemnation of evolutionary theory (to which I had become alerted as early as fifth grade at Fremont School by Mrs. Rooney). In our first semester of Jesuit philosophical studies at Mount St. Michael's, old Father Gaffney gave a series of lectures debunking evolutionary theory as only a "theory" based on the flimsiest of evidence and rampant imagination—little bones here and there, a few drawings on caves which were likely etched by young cave-children. All Jesuit philosophers and theologians agreed that the Book of Genesis was lucid on the fact that God had created Adam out of some kind of primal slime and had taken the care to directly breathe life into him, a divinely created soul.

From the time that Teilhard de Chardin was a young Jesuit, he spent his life among scientists on digs in Africa and Asia, where he came to develop his mystical synthesis of evolutionary theory and Christian theology, most popularly expressed in his book *The Phenomenon of Man*. A quiet scholarly Jesuit, he had died the year I graduated from Santa Clara and was buried in obscurity in New York, forbidden by his Jesuit superiors from publishing any of his papers. After his death, his scientist friends gathered his papers and published them in the secular world without the imprimatur of the Holy Office. Five years later, our dean Father Kossel, a sardonic converted apple-farmer from the Yakima Valley who had little use for Roman fussiness, surreptitiously smuggled the newly published

The Phenomenon of Man into the seminary and circulated it among a few of us.

My hands quivered with Teilhard's book as they had when I first read Rollo May. I thrilled at Teilhard's poetic praises of matter as the tangible visible manifestations of the invisible mind of God, and of the gradual unfolding of science and technology as Man's (sic) participation in the creative work of the divine, with the Cosmic Christ as the final goal of the meanderings of evolutionary adaptations, bestowing sense on the apparent randomness. His work was a blend of a truly deep feeling for the wonders of the material world, with an overlay of the most abstract theology joined with missionary zeal and founded on a scientized version of the City of God. This vision, he projected optimistically, would be the eventual result of a fertile marriage between Western science and Christianity, sweeping aside what he argued were anachronistic ideologies like Buddhism and Judaism.

Because Teilhard was a devout and brilliant Jesuit of my own era, willing to remain true to his vows despite repeated attacks on him by Roman authorities, I felt safer now as I allowed myself to open up to the world he described, finally free to indulge my interest in the natural sciences, which we had been taught to fear. I felt I could begin to enter the contemporary intellectual world with relish, just as the popularity of the poetry of the Jesuit Gerard Manley Hopkins allowed me to feel comfortable as a Jesuit in the literary world. After nearly thirty years of thinking of myself and humans in general as souls temporarily situated in uncomfortable, frail, and painful bodies, I began to get a feel for how our elaborate flights of theory and fantasy emanate from ancient material processes taking place within an unimaginably vast cosmos. I started to look differently and with more interest at the night sky and photomicroscopic images of living cells. For the first time in my life, I became interested in such banal things as rocks and slimes, and began to share Teilhard's vision of them as manifesting the earliest gestures of the divine. I now understood better why Albertus Magnus and Thomas Aquinas had been so interested in Aristotle's texts about the early origins of biology, and why the earliest Christian theologians wrote of the material universe as the first word of God. Exploring that word, they argued, was to contact the mind of God, a divine work.

✧

I know that this function of books in awakening me to a larger life is not by any means commonplace. My wife Barbara found her way into the larger world by intense physical activity and intimate contact with the Earth. She grew up on the plains of Texas in the climate described by Mary Karr's memoirs: addiction, abuse, the dashing of big hopes. Barbara broke the constraints of a suffering family and claustrophobic hometown by tough basketball, horseback riding by herself out on the plains, wilderness treks, river running, and lying on rocks. Only after she began to find hope through her body in intense physical explorations of the Earth was she drawn to poetry and literature to sustain and further her bodily discoveries.

Most of my students in the Somatics Graduate Studies Program, which I founded, are more like her: they first turned to dance, massage, and bodyworks, which expanded their sensitivities to the point where they wanted to learn more about the world revealed through books. Or they traveled the world, lived through life crises, went to jail for their politics. They lived with an intensity that led them directly into the vastness of human lives. But for me, an inactive and sickly child, afraid of the outdoors and vigorous bodily activities, I had to read myself into all that, on the intuition that the world around me was but a fragment of the real world. It was only through books that I found my way beyond the constricted conversations and pedagogies of the Sacramento Valley, the United

States, and even Western Europe. Reading prompted the desire to break out of a hometown notion of life devoted solely to having a family and making money, with a little Sunday religion thrown in for good measure. I was given other dreams of social justice, the joys of the vast human achievements throughout centuries of art, music, cuisine, architecture, philosophy, mystical practice, and political institutions.

Not all books have the capacity to achieve this opening of the soul. I have come to notice something about language that makes the *lectio* specifically *divina;* it's as if the words must have the feel of what early Christian theologians claimed about the Incarnation of Christ—Word made flesh, a Word that had to travel an infinitely long and difficult journey from Heaven to text through birth, sweat, and crucifixion. Mystics in the old wisdom traditions, poets, and writers of literate fiction and non-fiction open their readers to the vastness of the cosmos and the heart by wresting words from the muck of personal struggle, like Michelangelo in old age chiseling his agonized slaves out of enormous blocks of Carerra marble. Despite many differences of theme, field, tone, and original language, they all share hard-earned sentences, which communicate a sense that words and syntax are crucial steps in the development of nuanced thinking. They are not the results of rattling off what is on one's mind, easy castoffs, readymade from the racks of a Neiman Marcus New York editor or the more popular Target of the how-to industry. These are works of thinking through, describing, tracking the minute course of things. There is no thoughtless leap from one place to the other, where important details are glossed over. It is in the careful and often excruciating work of tracing back from here to there, filling in the gaps, going from the real present to the originally hoped-for, noticing the forgotten errors, the keen moves forward, that we might piece together a better way for us to live together.

8

Inspiration

ABSORPTION IN BOOKS, NO MATTER HOW VISIONARY, can easily draw the reading addict into a life of quiet narcissism. Where do we find the inspiration necessary to move out of that comfortable, though depressing, world of books into the roiling waters of daily life to deal with the daunting problems of interpersonal and planetary life? Though I was raised to think of inspiration as a symbolic or non-material reality, a lifetime of problems with breathing eventually led me to realize that inspiration is situated within a web of connections among our bodies, the larger world, and images of hope. Without the foundation of full-lunged and feet-feeling inspiration, the mind can easily rocket into a heady stratosphere of dissociated fanaticism fueled by abstract ideas, or collapse into an airless swamp of isolation and despair.

In my mother's garage, there are photos of me at twelve years old on the steps of my father's gun club near the Sutter Buttes with my hunting cap and jacket, my shotgun slung over my shoulder. Although the big smile across my face gives the impression that I was an ordinarily happy pubescent, I was in the midst of stifling bouts of asthma, which kept me incapacitated and isolated from the ordinary boyhood activities of my friends. Spasms gripped me in the damp early hours when we slogged out to the duck blinds to await our prey, or if I walked briskly for more than a hundred yards, or tried to play any sport. I dreaded going to bed at night, where I was awake for hours gasping for breath.

While I assume that most people take breathing for granted as much as the air around us, it has always been a daunting challenge for my father, my son, and me. My father died of sudden heart failure due, the doctors said, to years of stress from emphysema. My son began to show symptoms of asthma during his third year that intensified for several years until they abated as he has grown towards puberty. I spent the first twenty years of my life incapacitated by asthma, which left me with what doctors call subclinical emphysema characterized by reduced lung capacity and susceptibility to bronchial infections.

When I was growing up, I felt alone in my asthma because no one else suffered from it. Now it afflicts a rapidly increasing number of people in the Central Valley—three times the national average—exacerbated by the thick emissions from motor vehicles, mountains of cow manure, leaf-blowers, and unregulated heavy farm equipment. Throughout the long summer, the Valley newspapers report that the emergency rooms of the hospitals are filled with people undergoing respiratory crises. Children and seniors are warned not to go outside unless absolutely necessary. The notorious smog levels of the Los Angeles basin have long been surpassed by those in the Valley. The State of California Environmental Protection Agency has been conducting a variety of epidemiological studies that consistently point to the increased rates of asthma for children living within proximity of freeways, even in areas where the regional air is relatively clean.[15]

Sacramento has never been a great place for breathing. I grew up learning a certain wariness about dangers lurking in breezes or winds, an unease that still infects me. The Delta tule fogs of early winter, oozing up only about ten feet above the ground, render the air thick and dank like the atmosphere of the Belfast of Frank McCourt and his coughing family, and the Paris of Marcel Proust dying of asthma and pneumonia at fifty-six years old. An ordinary cold easily turns into bronchitis, which can hang on through the season. Because the air is always so foul during January and February, my mother and father in their later years would flee south to the Anza-Borrego Desert for a month or more. The one year they didn't, my father got deathly sick with bronchitis. In late summer and fall, long before smog caused by the proliferation of automobiles and diesels added to the problem, the Valley air would turn muddy brown as the rice stubble and dried grasses were burned to clear the fields for next season's planting. On still nights, it felt like being downwind of the dark volcanic ash gushing out of Kilauea on the Big Island.

The Valley is a welcoming corridor for the winds of the world. As a small child, I remember people around me speaking of the coming of the North Wind in the same fearful tones that they would soon use when spreading rumors that Japanese Zeroes and submarines were approaching the coast to attack us, or a new strain of influenza was invading from Hong Kong or Singapore. "The North Wind is kicking up" signaled danger to both mind and body. As it roared down the Valley from Mt. Shasta, following the course of the Sacramento River through Red Bluff and Williams across the levees into downtown where my grandfather and father had built their houses, it swept up clouds of dust and billows of pollens from the richest farmlands in the world, drying up everything, searing hot in the summer, bone-chilling in the winter. Unseasonable pneumonia or colds, migraine headaches, and depression were attributed to it. The southeast winds off the Mojave and the Mexican Sonora were also said to be dangerous. Street wisdom attributed to their hot dry tones ("positive ions" in a later lingo) mostly mental diseases of anger and impatience. Because they blew only a few days a year, people said they were less a problem than the chronic and relentless North. I still feel a heartfelt welcome when the winds blow warm and wet up from the South Pacific, redolent of nearly naked bodies dancing to sensual music on white-sand beaches, bringing the rushes of negative ions that help spirits lift.

My pediatric allergist diagnosed me as overly reactive to the allergenic pollens from the many trees and grasses that flourished in the Delta soil, and dust fine enough to penetrate our hermetically sealed house, breeding vicious mites in our carpets and bedding. But even more stifling was the turgid air in our house and car from my father's chain-smoking. He went through several packs a day until he was sixty years old and our family doctor said give it up or die. Both my grandfathers smoked until they died. I felt choked by the thick smoke in the car on our long drives.

During the ten years before my father died at seventy-eight, he was caught in a continual struggle to get a breath. It is not surprising that his breathing came to haunt his final years after a lifetime of working outside in heavy construction, beginning when he was eleven years old helping his father. He always lived in dust, the driest kind created by scraping off topsoil to make way for houses, pipelines, and highways. Like the coal miners in West Virginia and Wales, his lungs never got to enjoy the nurture afforded by fresh clean air, unpolluted by dust and cigarette smoke.

Warnings of his deterioration occurred as early as 1972 in his early sixties when he and my mother would drive to visit my family in Santa Fe, where my father was dangerously affected by the seven thousand feet of altitude. The first year he visited, he enthusiastically joined me scaling a ladder to lay a roof on a new room I was adding to our old adobe home. When he began to get very red in the face and short of breath, we rushed him to the emergency room at St. Vincent's Hospital, where the doctor said he was on the verge of a heart attack, but would be alright now if he took it easy. From then on, my parents drew out the length of their drives by two or three days, spending a night at five thousand feet in Albuquerque to get better adjusted. But he was never the same. When we would take walks around the high desert town, he would lag far behind us, shoulders hunched, face red, attention turned inward as if he were in danger of attack. His chronically edgy disposition, with his unpredictable outbursts of impatient rage and sarcasm, got even worse.

By the time I moved to San Francisco in 1981, his breathing was seriously crippled. I had a nineteenth-century "stick" Victorian house, some thirty stairs up from the sidewalk. As he ascended in slow steps and frequent stops, he looked like Tenzing Norgay clomping up the last hundred yards to the summit of Everest. It took him a good fifteen to twenty minutes to reach the top.

Six years before he died, my father was prescribed around-the-clock oxygen. Embarrassed by being leashed to a tank, he no longer wanted to have any social gatherings at the house and discouraged his friends from visiting, leaving him and my mother in virtual isolation. He withdrew into depression. Four years into this solitary confinement, he was admitted to Mercy Hospital for a gallbladder attack, where he happened into the care of two visiting specialists in pulmonary medicine—one French, the other Indian. They were assigned to monitor his breathing difficulties, while other physicians were treating his gallbladder. They had a cosmopolitan urbanity— friendly, joking easily with my father. Dr. Gandhi (an appropriate name for such a gentle and sensitive man) touched my father a lot, stroking his sad chest, holding his hand. They felt that the local physicians, because they were understandably unaware of the most recent developments in respiratory research, had unnecessarily confined him to daily oxygen. They prescribed a more sophisticated course of a new generation of anti-inflammatories without the oxygen tanks. From the time he left the hospital until his sudden death two years later, my father once again welcomed friends to the house, and he traveled with my mother, even as far as Kauai. He was about as happy as I had ever known him, an important example for me of how breathing and hope are linked. He and I recovered a quiet peace with one another that I had not enjoyed with him since I was a teenager.

The changes prescribed by the Indian and French pulmonary specialists were the first signals of a basic change in the scientific understanding of the nature of asthma and its treatment. Up until then, it was thought to be primarily a dysfunction in muscle constriction, something like repetitive motion injuries, where the bronchii and alveoli tighten up inappropriately in response to allergens. My doctors prescribed inactivity and relaxation, as they once did for so-called hysterical women like Charlotte Perkins Gillman in mid-life depression. Running, going out in the ill winds, talking too much, playing sports, traveling to high altitudes were to be avoided. Standard medications were antihistamines and sedatives designed to create a therapeutic lassitude in the body; they took away any urge to do intense activities and diminished physical energy. During the past two or three decades, scientists have found that asthma is primarily an inflammatory reaction, an inappropriate auto-immune response to allergens, like certain kinds of arthritis. Anti-inflammatory steroids and genetically engineered drugs that inhibit the cascade of self-defeating responses to the allergens are now the primary medications. The goal of treatment is to permit, even encourage, an ordinarily active life, especially in children, where lung development through sports and intense activity is thought to be helpful in reducing the power of the chronic disease, even allowing some children to outgrow it.

I had a foretaste of that change in therapeutic philosophy when I was a junior in college. I had joined the wrestling team because my closest friends devoted all their time to it. But the price of being with my friends in this intimate muscular embracing was that I had to do the daily workout of running a mile around the track on the football field, even when it was raining or on the coldest windy days of winter. Up until that time, I avoided running because the wheezing would come on just as soon as I started playing a game of hide-and-go-seek or sandlot baseball. In high school, I avoided all strenuous physical activities except golf, whose leisurely pace didn't provoke attacks. By contrast, I found that the daily wrestling regimen, even when I wheezed to the point of choking, effected the first permanent break in the course of the periodic crises. Although I wheezed heavily all the way, I made it, and I began to realize that I might just as well do such activities as not. I felt healthier and less isolated from my friends, and survived the winter without bronchitis.

This was the first of many experiences that led me to realize the importance of the physical body in responding to the needs of the soul. Breathing was not only about oxygen and blood; it gave me the inspiration to participate more fully in life; it opened up a more human world.

In 1990, shortly before the demise of the Soviet Union, I spent three days visiting a thousand-year-old Russian Orthodox monastery on the Estonian border near Pskov. I was there with an elder Russian neuropsychiatrist from the Pavlov Institute in Leningrad (now St. Petersburg) whose life work had been research in altered states of consciousness among various cultures in the far-flung Soviet empire: the Buddhist monks of Buryat, the shamans in Kamchatka and the Siberian North, and the scattered Orthodox mystics who had survived the purges. This monastery was one of the few that had not been destroyed by Stalin, and the monks there were still practicing the ancient techniques of hesychasm, popularly identified with the Jesus prayer, a coordination of breath, and repetitive short prayers. We happened to be there for the major feast of their liturgical year in honor of the prophet Elijah, the one whom God visited not in a tornado or an earthquake but in a gentle breeze, and who was the only biblical personage to escape death, carried away in a whirlwind to Heaven by the fiery chariot drawn by fiery horses, from then on being a source of believers' hopes for overcoming death. The abbot was a gorgeous, elegantly tall man. He excused himself three times during the day to change into subtly different cuts of black silk robes signifying, he said, changes in the cycle of the day; and he constantly fingered the heavy gold and ruby cross hung from a gold chain about his neck, which he said his spiritual teacher had passed on to him. He explained that their monastic rituals had the goal of transforming their bodies from what Paul the Apostle called "meat" (Greek: *sarx*), a death-bound physical muck, into a luminous immortal body (Greek: *soma*) promised by Jesus's resurrection from the dead and by Elijah's physical immortality. Their basic transformative practice was breathing, cultivated in their hours of chant and especially in their physical work of maintaining the very large institution, with its immaculately kept gardens, orchards, machinery, icon studio, book bindery, and many other crafts required by a self-supporting community, a lush island in the midst of Soviet desolation. He took us to the forge to visit one of their senior religious teachers, a blacksmith in his eighties. He was shaping hot iron, in and out of the forge, maneuvering like a dancer with his very concentrated breath and gestures, his face radiant and kind as he received us. At the end of our visit to the monastery, I invited the abbot to join us at Camaldoli in our seminar on the relation between the body and spirituality. He reared up to his full height, seemingly shocked that we would have mentioned such a topic in his presence, and said that he had no interest at all in the human body.

Twenty-five years earlier, I had received teachings similar to the Russian Orthodox views about the immortal significance of human flesh from our Jesuit Master of Novices Father Healy, which I realize only in retrospect set in motion a long life of interest in studying methods of body cultivation. A first-generation Irish-American,

Father Healy stood out as peculiar even among the odd community of celibate priests. He was austere and cold, rarely smiling except in sarcasm when scolding one or another of us for inappropriate behavior, such as exchanging a friendly word in English when Latin or silence was required. Despite an ascetic denigration of sensual pleasures of any sort, he was obsessed with bodily transformation, reading to us daily from the books on physical transformation in the lives of the saints by the Jesuit scholar of mysticism Herbert Thurston. Like the Russian abbot, he argued that our mystical practices were aimed at the transformation of our flesh into immortal bodies. Because of the eternal significance of our bodies, he read books on psychosomatic medicine, hypnotism, and diet, even phrenology, which he used as a diagnostic tool to see if we were fit for the priesthood. He taught us meditation practices grounded in sensory awareness; and we practiced deliberate postures in meditation associated with desired states of consciousness. He enticed us to saintly virtue with promises of the kinds of bodily transformation that occur in the documentation of the lives of the saints: teleportation, elongation, levitation, sweet-smelling body odor, and ultimately an immortal body of blissful pleasure or excruciating pain.

One of our main and constant practices was to focus on our breathing during the activities of the day, coordinating it with brief prayers, like the Jesus prayer.

Though these teachings may seem esoterically bizarre, they are rigorously logical conclusions of the long tradition of Roman Catholic theology. The biblical foundation for the teaching was St. Paul's assertion that if Christ did not rise from the dead in an immortal body—the pledge of our immortality in the flesh—then all our other beliefs are in vain. At its most contentious peak during the Protestant Reformation, Catholic theologians made it utterly clear that what divided them from the Reformers was the belief in the divinity of the material world. In stark and violent contrast to Luther and Calvin's notions, the Catholic theology of the Eucharist, for example, held that during the mass, the plain bread was literally, NOT symbolically, changed by the priest into the real flesh of the risen Christ, and that the persons who consumed that flesh were themselves being transformed into that immortal body.

There was, however, a profound contradiction between the ascetic climate of our life, which proscribed the least dalliance with sensuality, and the mystical teachings of breathing and sensory awareness. Practical guidance about sacred embodiment articulated by Father Healy and subsequent spiritual advisers was paradoxically disembodied, with the emphasis being put on techniques for turning attention away from our physical impulses towards sacred thoughts and images. Because we had no instruction in actual steps for withdrawing our attention from the more familiar outer world of objects and thoughts to focus on the depths of our physical bodies, I filed those teachings away in some ethereal closet, neither physical nor spiritual, until I eventually encountered secular teachers who knew how to lead one into the depths of bone, breath, and gesture.

One such person was Ilsa Middendorf, born in 1910 outside Berlin, where she still lives and directs her training institute. When she was only a young girl, she had a visionary experience in the garden of her family home in which she heard a voice calling to her: "You have to breathe." She didn't know what to make of that experience until her adolescent years, when she became a student of the Gymnastic movement that spread throughout Western Europe beginning in the nineteenth century as a reaction to intellectualized approaches to dance and exercise. The founders of this movement used music, art, and image to teach students to exploit the wide-ranging possibilities for personal expression latent in the body. It was there that her earlier vision began to make sense and she embarked on a lifetime of examining how one actually breathes—where in the body, how long a cycle, where restricted, what happens in response to touch and word, over long periods of time in response to the changing emotional climate of one's life, and particularly how attention to breathing changes it in an expansive energizing way. She helps people develop an individual profile revealed through these sustained studies into what she calls "the breathing self."

In the course of developing her method of work, she drew from Asian sources, particularly the Tibetan Buddhist and Chinese Taoist heritages. Her method, however, differs in at least two significant regards. She thinks of herself as the bearer of a characteristically Western experimental attitude that holds in question any preconceived notions about breathing:

> I was in China and noticed that they often worked with breathing in a guided way, by will. The Tibetan system was the same. The most important difference between those kinds of methods and ours is the feeling that we want to follow the law of breathing. We are into this law—not above or beside it. We want to know: what does *breathing* mean? That is a very important differentiation. These other systems I studied may have suggested some directions, but my work comes entirely from my own explorations.[16]

Connected intimately with that radical experimentalism is a consciously feminist challenge to patriarchal culture:

> All the yoga ways of breathing come out of the male way. The Eastern way of thinking is to find god in one direction, in a male way. "The way is directed. I go there and I have to go; I must go." This male way of being needs will. When this is the basis, the breathing is under the law of the will.[17]

Middendorf barely survived the War with her young child living outside Berlin while her husband was inscripted in the German army and then killed on the Russian front. The historical matrix of her work, shared by many other teachers of her generation, gave a particular cast to body cultivation that is crucial for sorting out the difference between hope, missionary zeal, and utopian fanaticism. She and other pioneers of similar bodily practices survived the ravages only with great pain and personal loss. They saw firsthand in the regimes of Hitler, Stalin, and Mao how closely mass insanity was associated with an emphasis on bodily health, strength, and purity. With their poignant knowledge that attention to the body has no automatic connection with humane values, they directly addressed the difference between a superficial approach to the body with the aim of making it a well-oiled instrument for secular or religious goals that come from elsewhere, and an approach that leads to nurturing inherent and often neglected capacities of the body for such humane qualities as sensitivity, courage, and kindness.

My decades of studying with such teachers has made me feel that tendencies towards utopian fanaticism are connected with an alienation from a more substantial sense of self, grounded in bodily sensations. In the popular mind, Middendorf breath work and similar methods of gaining intimacy with our bodily being are typically confused with techniques for healing dysfunctions, learning how to relax, and keeping fit. The innovators of these various embodiment practices, however, saw them primarily as ways to familiarize ourselves with the full significance of our situation as blood-filled, oxygen-needing, joint-moving creatures sustained by a natural world. Fanaticism, both religious and secular, is fueled by consciousness uprooted from body awareness, lost in mad fantasy. The long-term practice of these embodiment methods lessens the overbalanced emphasis on some imagined future life—whether here or in a fantasized eternal realm—and helps redirect our attention to those people close to us, the smells of the air about us, the noises of the street.

9

Birth and Death

W

HAT COULD BE SIMPLER AND MORE OBVIOUS than noticing and accepting that we breathe and move our joints? How is it that this simple awareness of ourselves as geneticneuromuscularphysiological and bony beings seems such a difficult, even controversial activity? Major clues to this puzzle can be found in widespread attitudes towards the outer limits of our existence in birth and death.

When my wife Barbara was pregnant with our son, we took part in a ritual performed by a Tibetan rimpoche. At the gathering afterwards, we asked him if there were Tibetan practices surrounding birth like the well-known ones prescribed for death. He replied that rituals for both events are the same, because one is being reborn as one is dying; birth is simply the last of the various stages of the journey facilitated by the rituals described in *The Book of the Dead.* Although his answer made logical Buddhist sense, there was something about it that didn't seem quite right. As in Christianity, the rituals and sacred art surrounding death in the Buddhist tradition are far more prevalent than those about birth: meditations on corpses, funeral rituals, final rites, paintings depicting skeletal beings and the decay of flesh. There are striking exceptions in depictions of the birth of Jesus and of the Buddha, but these are few by comparison.

Before the Vatican II reforms of the 1960s, death and its aftermath were at the core of Catholic theology and spiritual practice.

At St. Francis Church, we altar boys coveted assignments to funerals, especially the long and elegant high masses with their gilded black vestments, long chants, hand-wrought silver holy water sprinklers, and incensers on gold chains. In addition to getting us out of class for a couple of hours, their music and color provided as much entertainment as any Hollywood musical.

The most dramatic event of the liturgical cycle in that era was the ritualization of Christ's death on Good Friday. The celebration of the resurrection on Easter Sunday paled by comparison to its ancient chants and choreographies. The Good Friday mass was called the Mass of the Presanctified since the hosts used for Holy Communion were not consecrated then but on the day before at the Holy Thursday mass. After the solemn intoning of the *Gloria in excelsis* at the beginning of the mass, all the statues in the church were covered with purple cloths and the candles extinguished. The main priest donned a special black silk vestment. The entire passion of St. John was chanted, with various priests taking the parts of the narrator, Jesus, Pontius Pilate, and Herod. The congregation would take the few parts assigned to the crowd, chanting at the right moment, *Crucifige eum*, Crucify Him.

This emphasis on death is not so hard to grasp. Until the twentieth century, when longevity doubled and tripled, an increase more rapid than during any previous time in history, the struggle just to stay alive was of momentous concern. Life was short and hard; birth was only a tentative moment whose outcome had to be worked out in constant danger of widespread disease and violence. A large proportion of newborns did not survive infancy; those who did often died young.

In our old Sacramento neighborhood, we lived in the midst of undertakers and graveyards. The Gormley Funeral Home was around the corner from us on Capitol Avenue, where it still stands. Three generations of their family, descendants of Bishop Manogue, the first bishop of Sacramento, have buried all my grandparents and my father. The Culjis parlor, where many of the family friends had their obsequies, was a few blocks away. My mother's parents and her Irish relatives are buried in the old St. Mary's cemetery next to Christian Brothers High School on Broadway. Great-Grandmother Lucy, her daughter Auntie, and her three daughters are buried in the nearby Masonic cemetery, next to Odd Fellows where my father was buried. His parents and my uncles are buried a little further out in East Lawn.

Death seemed to dog the heels of my mother and grandfather Joe Hanlon. It always seemed to me that something of them was missing, suspended back somewhere in time. Joe's mother had died giving him birth, and then his wife Rose died of breast cancer as a young woman. He always seemed to be living back there somewhere.

Something of my mother's soul seems to be still hovering back there, too, on that day just before her thirteenth birthday, when she found her mother lifeless, a tragic surprise since no one had explained the seriousness of her mother's illness. Eighty years later, she still often alludes to that day, telling us how, after her mother's death, she would get up in the middle of the night to check that her father was still breathing, and when she would go away with friends overnight, she would make an effort to call home to see that he was still alive. When any of us venture too far from the safety of home, she fears that we may not return.

Grandpa Joe's and my mother's suspension in the past had a mysterious quality. I have known many other people who have endured far greater numerical losses—Holocaust families, great-grandchildren of slaves, refugees from Cambodia and El Salvador, people who endured rape, torture, loss of home, and many family members—who continue to go on creating a new present, often with joy and imagination. When I speculate about why my family members were so trapped back in time, I imagine that at least one factor was their Irish Jansenist version of Catholicism. Unlike the slave Christianity of redemption and resurrection, described at Camaldoli by Vincent and Rosemarie Harding, their Irish-Roman-based religion was centered on death and guilt.

Theologians have lamented the bifurcation of early Christianity into Western Roman Catholicism and Eastern Orthodoxy. In the sacred music, art, and architecture of the West, Jesus's Passion and Crucifixion gained central place. Its images dominate every altar and bell-tower, the walls of the churches are ringed by the Stations of the Cross, the great paintings and sculptures are of Jesus writhing in suffering, or lying dead on his mother's lap. In Istanbul, St. Petersburg, and Kiev, the glorious risen Christ covers the great domes in gilded mosaics, surrounded by the heavenly hosts and the saints in their immortal bodies transformed triumphant over death, looking down listening to the joyful chants of the Orthodox hymnals.

Our Jesuit mystical training was based on the Spiritual Exercises by the Basque Ignatius Loyola, formulated in a land rife with feudal terrorism and the violence of the Spanish Inquisition. This famous spiritual regimen, which shaped many European princes, bishops, and popes, is divided into four "weeks," whose actual number of days is determined by the spiritual progress of the exercitant. The first week is devoted to meditating on the Original Sin of Adam and Eve, which redirected humanity from Edenic bliss towards hard labor, suffering, and death. It took the extreme torture and murder of Jesus to right this tragic deviation. Our personal sins, it was said, added to the intensity of Jesus's suffering by some kind of spiritual time warp. Ignatius gave instructions that no one was to leave that "week" until he gained the special state of repentance for his sins based on tearfully felt grief for causing such pain to the beloved Jesus, rather than on fear of Hell. The first step towards that "perfect contrition" was gaining a literal taste for the putrid airs of Hell and Purgatory, a vivid imagination of what it will feel like to have one's immortal body eternally seared because of our furtive genital touches and lying words. Many people, Ignatius reasoned, will spend their entire lives returning only to the meditations of that "week" in their spiritual practices, attempting to reach that desired point where they weep for how their seemingly trivial actions have broken the heart of the Lord of the Cosmos. In most cases, only a few exercitants got to spend more than six or seven days on the last three "weeks" of the thirty-day period meditating on Christ's life and resurrection, the bliss of Heaven, and the proper way to shape one's life to serve Christ.

In our inaugural thirty-day retreat as Jesuit novices, I was horrified to find myself in a world that was more medieval than I had bargained for, nothing like the community of intellectual renaissance men I had met at Santa Clara. On the first morning we were seated in the Novitiate lecture hall, quietly waiting for our Father Master Healy's typically ghostly entrance. He would glide slowly down the side of the room, his long soutane swishing against the floor, eyes cast down as prescribed by Ignatius' "Rules of Modesty." But in his hands this morning were a small corded whip and two sets of spiked chains, which he placed on the table in front of him. These, he said, are among the ways we identify with the suffering and death of Christ, and join with him in repentance for human sinfulness. He explained that on specified days one or another sign would be posted on the bulletin board: *Flagellatio* signified that after litanies in the chapel at night we were to return to our cubicles and drop our pants and underpants. At the sound of a bell, the lights would be shut off and we were to begin whipping our buttocks until the second bell rang, after which we were to don our pajamas and prepare for bed. He demonstrated by whipping the palm of his hand. The intensity and speed of the blows, he explained, would depend on the fervor of our desire to identify with the whipped body of Jesus. *Catenulae* on the bulletin board meant that when we arose at 5 a.m., we were to wrap one spiked chain around our bicep, the other around our thigh, and wear them through morning visit, meditation, and mass. The pain inflicted by the spikes would give us a better sense of what Jesus endured with his crown of thorns. He then proceeded to give an introductory lecture on the use of severe physical penances in the history of the great Jesuit saints, a theme that would come up in the many biographies I would read over the years. In every case, the saint—Robert Bellarmine, Aloysius Gonzaga, Stanislaus Kostka, Ignatius himself—outdid any sadomasochistic fantasies, whipping themselves for long periods, wearing hairshirts, starving themselves nearly to death. Our Master's contemporary hero was the Irish Jesuit Willy Doyle, who was renowned for getting up every morning well before dawn, running naked into the chill Irish air and hurling himself into a pond, then diving into a patch of brambles on his way back to meditation and a large Irish breakfast.

My heart sank. Inspired by Santa Clara professors, who were cosmopolitan, literate, and radiant with humanistic idealism, I had entered the Jesuits feeling that I was escaping the constricted world of commerce and family. Now I found that I had moved backwards in time into an even more constricted medieval world.

That night, as the lights went out and we dropped our pants and began whipping, visualizing the naked Christ being flailed at the stake, hearing the sighs of my brothers I found myself getting an erection and was transported into a new kind of confusing pleasure. When I mentioned this to the Master in my daily colloquy, he looked out the window with his blank rock-cod-like expression and slowly replied that the brother of St. Theresa of Avila wrote that he had the same problem when he was a missionary in Brazil. I left his room bewildered, not knowing whether his koan-like response implied permission to keep enjoying the sexual stimulations along with the penitential pain, or that I should volunteer for the Brazilian missions.

The major meditations of that week were intricate sensual imaginings of Jesus's final days and imagined scenarios of our own death. Of the several methods of meditation our Master of Novices taught us, the "Application of the Senses" stands out as having a lasting influence on my life's work, giving me a feel for the power of active imagination rooted in bodily experience. The method involved selecting an event in the Bible and applying each of the five senses to that event: visualizing the details, hearing the sounds, smelling, getting a feel for the textures, tasting. We spent days learning to sense in minute detail the scourge striking Jesus's back, the thorns pricking his brow, the agony of dragging his heavy cross through the streets of Jerusalem up the steep slope to Calvary, the nails punching through his hands and feet, his thirst as he hung there jeered at by the crowds.

We spent two or three entire days applying that method to the contemplation of Hell. Here is how Ignatius wrote it:

> ... see in imagination the vast fires, and the souls enclosed, as it were, in bodies of fire.

> ... hear the wailing, the howling, cries, and blasphemies against Christ our Lord and against his saints.

> ... with the sense of smell to perceive the smoke, the sulphur, the filth, and corruption.

... to taste the bitterness of tears, sadness, and remorse of conscience.

... with the sense of touch to feel the flames which envelop and burn the souls.[18]

I was so terrified by these imaginings that one night my cubical-mates had to drag me down screaming from a wall I was climbing in my sleep, trying to get out of a high transom above my bed.

Like participants in Stanislaus Grotowski's theater experiments in Poland, we were to imagine in intricate detail various scenarios of how we might die: the exact events that led to our dying—car accident, cancer, mugging, heart attack, stroke—the people around our death bed, what they thought of us, our sensory and emotional feelings as we approached the end, even to the point of being in the coffin and hearing the clods beating down on the lid and seeing the expressions of our loved ones and friends as they walked away from the grave. One had to devote one's meditations to those themes for as long as it took to reach the desired feelings of repentance and identification with Christ Crucified, the proof of which was tears. I never reached this point, so the Master instructed me to stay with these meditations on sin, Hell, and the death of Jesus.

When I lived in Santa Fe many years later, I had the opportunity to take part in some of the inner rituals of the Penitentes, a lay religious brotherhood that had taken root among the Spanish peasants who originally settled in the Sangre de Cristo Mountains some four hundred years ago when there were no priests available to carry on the Catholic practices. The now fashionable religious art displayed in the salons of Santa Fe is crafted by the Penitentes, whose long isolation in their high-country villages produced a unique tradition of sculpture, painting, music, and architecture.

The striking thing about the liturgical cycle of the Penitentes was that it ended dramatically and abruptly with the Good Friday processions through the rocky high desert, during which the men beat themselves, knelt on the rocky ground, some even mounting their own crosses to suffer near the point of death. Each village has a meeting house called the *Morada*. On Easter Sunday, the *Moradas* were closed while the Brothers went to mass at the local parish church. None of the handcarved images of Jesus that adorn the *Moradas* depict the Resurrection, only the various tortures and crucifixion, in bloody detail.

The austerities of the Brotherhood seem bizarre unless you think of how difficult it has been to settle and survive in the high desert and mountain ranges with extreme temperature variations, wild winds, and short growing seasons; the aesthetic mirrors and ritualizes the environment. Their emphasis on suffering and death goes hand-in-hand with a vibrant compassion manifested in rigorous demands for service to the community. The Brothers care for villagers in need, children, the aged, the sick. In places where the Brotherhood is weak or gone, the communities have fallen apart, the elderly are bereft, the young form gangs.

One might interject here that Christianity clearly puts the birth of Jesus at the center of its worship, with Christmas and the arts of the Nativity as widespread as the liturgies of the Crucifixion. And yet, on closer inspection, neither the theology nor the art has to do with birth as we ordinary humans know it. The details of how Mary gave birth to Jesus was one of the liveliest, even violent, theological debates of the first three centuries of Christian theology. Theologians had to weave complex threads of fragile reason to synthesize a number of seemingly irreconcilable dogmas:

1. Labor pains, according to the authoritative reading of Genesis, were the curse placed on Eve and her progeny for biting the apple. The Lord God said to the woman:

"I will multiply the pangs of your childbearing; in pain shall you bring forth your children." (Genesis 3:16) Because Mary, the Immaculate Conception, was the only woman not to inherit Eve's penalties, it was not possible for her to have those pains.

2. Mary was a virgin before and after birth. In that old way of thinking, virgins (who were not typically gymnasts or horsewomen) had their hymen intact, so Jesus had to have come out of Mary's body without rupturing it.

3. He could not be Caesarean born, a painful curse to which only the heirs of sinful Adam and Eve are subject.

By the time of Augustine of Hippo in the fifth century, the Virgin Birth had taken on the basic dogmatic structure that would be passed on to me by Franciscan Father John in my weekly catechism classes, and then by my Jesuit teachers. The birth of Jesus was not at all like human births. In contrast to what is portrayed in the rituals and meditations surrounding Jesus's death, which repeat and stretch out every agonizing moment between the Last Supper and the taking down of his body from the cross some twenty-four hours later, his birth takes place in a timeless, bodiless realm; it just happens. One moment he was comfortably riding in the womb, conceived by the spiritual semen of the Holy Spirit penetrating one of Mary's superhuman ova. The next moment he appeared miraculously and painlessly on the straw for all to worship, having undergone no struggles out of the birth canal, nor uttered any cries at the shock and effort.

The uniqueness of the Christian tradition of Jesus's birth stands out in stark relief if the thousands of sculptures and paintings of Mary and Baby Jesus—rosy-cheeked, calm and blissful, not a whiff of hard labor or infant agony—are compared with sculptures of certain African tribes or of India, which portray the various stages of a woman's bringing the baby through her vaginal opening.

In my early days of the Jesuit Novitiate, I discovered just how seriously the doctrine of the Virgin Birth is held. Our curriculum included a weekly lecture by a theologian from the nearby Jesuit school of theology in the Santa Cruz mountains. One week it was to be a lecture on the Virgin Birth by Father Farrahar, known as "Rughead" because he coifed his sparse kinky dark hair by allowing its few thick patches to grow long enough to stretch them across his bald pate. There was a question box in the back of the lecture hall into which our Master of Novices encouraged us to place in advance any questions we might have about the topic. Unmonitored questions from the floor were not permitted lest anyone dare broach a forbidden topic in public. Just having graduated from Santa Clara University where our final class was a notoriously steamy senior class on graphic sexuality designed to prepare us for Catholic marriage, I dropped a slip in the box asking how he, as a modern theologian, made sense of a birth that did not occur through the vaginal canal. Father Farrahar gave his lecture and responded to a few written questions without any mention of mine.

Later that week, I received the dreaded piece of paper called the *"Vult"* (from the Latin *"Pater Magister **vult** videre te,"* or "Father Master **wants** to see you"). When I entered Father Healy's office, he was holding the slip of paper with my question written on it. Looking from it to me, he said that he was wondering if it was possible for me to continue at the Novitiate since this question indicated rebellious tendencies to question the authority of the Pope, a cardinal offense for a member of the Order who made up the inner circle of the Pope's defenders. His narrowed eyes and just a hint of a sardonic grin must have been what many men and women faced before they were assigned to racks and pinions for similar peccadilloes. I rapidly concocted some excuse of how troubled I had been in college about discussion on this topic and just had hoped to get some clarity. He continued to look at me without changing his expression until I finished, when he cast his eyes back down on the note and told me I could leave now. I was shaking all over.

It was not until the late 1970s that I began to get some inkling about a different kind of balance between birth and death. It happened when I sat out the death of a woman in her seventies who had been a Rolfing client and friend. In 1940, she and her late husband had homesteaded a hundred acres in the arid badlands outside Española, New Mexico, where she spent her life in the one-room adobe house they built. Three years before she died, in the course of her series of Rolfing sessions with me, a tumor in her abdomen was found to be malignant and fast growing. She chose to forego any advanced medical technologies of surgery, chemotherapy, or radiation, in the spirit of her life-long simple living on the land. Her physician was a medical homeopath, who cared for her to the end, giving her morphine only when it became necessary to relieve her increasing pain. I was fortunate to be there for her final hours as she lay on her bed receiving her old friends. It was sunset. She lay frail and cradled in the arms of the young man who had helped care for her garden, with a big pot of posole cooking on the wood stove to feed the continuous stream of visitors. The liveliness in her limbs, eyes, and facial expressions seemed to be slowly receding from the room until it was just gone. Her old dog began to howl.

Out of nowhere, I had the thought that this moment seemed like a birth, an odd thought given that I had never witnessed a birth, not even in films. I had deliberately avoided the many occasions when I might have. I knew abstractly from anatomy studies the bare outline of the process, but I had never read about actual births or talked with friends or clients about their experiences. It was twenty years later, when my first child was born just before my sixtieth birthday, that I could make sense of that eerie connection.

As I was approaching my fifty-fifth birthday, deep in depression about both my life and the world, I had the sense that I had shaped my life so that I would never have my own child. I had helped raise three wonderful children, whose lives have remained close to mine, though they are well into adulthood with children of their own, and a loving father who has always been very active in their lives. I had been through two marriages, ending in sorrow. Then I met and fell in love with Barbara who, in middle age, had never had a child. After our first two years together, we decided that we wanted to try to get pregnant. When we succeeded, I felt a certain terror underlying the intense joy. Birth felt dangerous, life-threatening, but more than that, totally unknown in its actual details, as missing from my imagination as they were in accounts of the Virgin Birth. In the early months, I spent time with the midwives who were generous in explaining in great detail the birthing process, the possible dangers, the ways of responding to those dangers, gradually helping me get familiar with a region of existence I had never faced. One particular phrase they used became like a repetitive mantra during the nine months: women's bodies have known how to accomplish this process successfully for millions of years.

When I was discussing my fears with a friend who had two young sons, and told him that I had been born Caesarean, he gave me a small, simply written book: Jane English's *A Different Doorway: Adventures of a Caesarean Born*.[19] She, like myself, had long been involved with the Esalen Community where she became attracted to Stanislaus Grof's Holotropic Breath Work, a practice involving guided imagery, structured breathing exercises, and music; one of the goals of the methodology is to deal with traumas arising at birth. He had designed the process to duplicate his earlier but now outlawed use of psychedelic drugs to conduct people through what he believed to be well-defined developmental challenges in an archetypal journey from womb into the world, in stages he synthesized from the theories of Freud, Rank, Adler, and Jung. Despite her attraction to what he was teaching, she, like myself, could never really respond to the work. As she spoke with him about her difficulties with the process, he wondered if a Caesarean birth might dictate different symbolic stages in the birth experience from what he had organized, and encouraged her to investigate this question.

Jane attended a Caesarean birth, which she describes in detail in the first pages of her book. Though written simply and dispassionately, even with a positive tone, the details felt so chilling that they made me cry. Something about the description of opening the woman, clamping back the folds, suctioning the nose of the baby and dangling it by its ankles, sewing back the woman, brought me to envision what it might have been like for my mother and me in a way I had never dared imagine.

Jane distinguishes non-labor from labor Caesareans in which the surgery occurs after the mother has already begun labor. She argues that the two experiences are likely to be quite different. A Caesarean performed when labor has already begun has the commonsense quality of any rescue; the process has already gotten underway, yet help is needed. In the non-labor Caesarean, which she had, the collaborative movements of child and mother to initiate birth are severely interrupted from the outside.

I happened to be visiting my mother just after reading this book, when Barbara was about six months pregnant. With the details of Jane's book in my mind, I was able to ask my mother detailed questions about my own birth for the first time ever. All she had told me until that point was that I was the first person in our family not to be born at home and that I was delivered at 8:30 a.m. She had to go for a Caesarean to Mercy Hospital, conducted by the Sisters of Mercy who were her high school teachers. In 1934, doctors commonly judged women of her size (4'-11") as lacking a sufficiently large pelvic opening to deliver naturally, and they believed that once she had a Caesarean she could not get pregnant again without great danger. Like many ephemeral medical dogmas, this too was eventually altered, but she and my father had sadly given up their dream of having more children. And I was left with the problems of being an only child.

Sitting quietly with my mother at her breakfast table, I asked if she went into labor before the surgery. She said, "Oh, no! The doctor didn't want to take any chances of that happening. He was going on vacation around the time that you were expected, so he scheduled it a couple of weeks early, just to be sure." Strange to say, that was the first time in my life that I adverted to the fact that my birth-time of 8:30 a.m. was determined more by the doctor's schedule than by a natural process. Not too long ago, my mother gave me the bill for that birth, which I have framed: for the surgery and two weeks' stay in the hospital, it amounted to $136.23.

That afternoon we visited my aunt Gladys. She and my mother began reminiscing about the births and infancy of me and my four cousins. They joked about the rigid scheduling the nurses and doctors prescribed. In the hospital, we would be brought to them exactly every three hours for breast-feeding and then promptly returned to the nursery, whether we were asleep or awake, hungry or not. At home for the first few months, they slavishly followed that schedule in nursing us. I sat stunned as I listened.

When I went to bed that evening, I found myself breaking into sobs that persisted for a long time. I had nightmarish images of primal interference, Dr. Savarein cutting into my comfortable womblike world, dragging me out into the bright cold, people cleaning me up, dragging me to and fro, constantly interrupting my sleep or failing to respond to my cries of hunger as they followed an abstract

schedule of nursing and contact with my mother, a relentless series
of interruption into the years when I always felt interfered with by
parents, doctors, priests, teachers, psychotherapists, friends, loved
ones, editors and agents, until I automatically bristled when anyone
made a move to get near me, always on guard against intrusions of
whatever sort, real or imagined.

As the grief subsided, it was clearer to me why I have given my
life to exploring various avenues of bodily manipulation and awareness, trying to recover the lost hiatuses in the primal journey from
womb to world.

My son's birth was anticipated for the last week of February
1994. On the slopes of Mount Tamalpais where we live, that season
is rainforest lush. As the days approached, with the baby kicking
vigorously and Barbara feeling very good, we took long walks in
the canyons and along the beaches. February passed into the first
and second week of March. We were now at the outer limit of the
fourteen days which medical authorities allowed the midwives to
do home deliveries. Thanks to our ob-gyn, who herself had given
birth only three months earlier, she sanctioned Barbara and our
midwives to have a long weekend beyond the two weeks to see if
she could bring the birth to completion without going to the hospital on Monday morning, March 14, for induced labor. The contractions began on Friday. Because her vaginal opening remained
at four centimeters all day Friday, Saturday, and Sunday, the midwives called it "useless" labor, even though Barbara, intimately familiar with her body rhythms, felt that everything was developing
in what seemed to be an appropriate manner. But the contractions
during Friday and Saturday nights robbed her of sleep to the point
where by Sunday afternoon she felt she was dangerously losing
the stamina she would need to accomplish the birth. During a

conversation with our ob-gyn around nine o'clock in the evening, she told Barbara she had two choices: either come to the hospital then and take morphine to get through the night, or take a hot bath and a glass of wine (after having abstained from alcohol during the previous nine months). With a sentence that we often remember, Barbara said, "I'm not dying; I'm having a baby," and chose the wine and bath. As she sat in the tub, I brought her a glass of very expensive zinfandel given us months earlier by a friend. Within moments, it was as if a Chinese dragon had entered the house, and Barbara, like one of Mayumi Oda's goddesses astride a giant carp, mounted and rode it with an awesome divine skill and courage. I suddenly found myself at the unfamiliar juncture between birth and death, the boundaries of another world, that I had sensed earlier when I sat with a dying woman. By 11:30, when the midwives finally arrived, our son's hairy head was appearing in the cavity, and at 12:11, he slipped right out into my waiting hands.

Perhaps it was because I had lived so long by the time my son was born, and had gotten used to feeling myself radically alone in the universe, taking for granted a certain bleakness, that my intimate contact with the birth effected such a dramatic shift in my sense of self. I felt suddenly plunged into the heart of the human community. My former school classmates, who had children at more commonplace ages, tell me how distant the births of their children were as they sat long hours in the lobby of hospitals hearing only distant cries of women, not knowing which were their wives. And also, how their adulthood was shaped from the outset by their being fathers. For me, by contrast, those brief three hours of riding alongside Barbara as she bucked the volcanic contractions, seeing our son's dark curly hair appear, and the moment of catching him emerging and cutting his umbilical cord rank among the most vivid experiences of my life.

In the light of those nine months and the final dramatic hours, I saw how death-centered was much of the perennial philosophy and theology that had shaped my thinking, understandable given the profound hardships our ancestors had to bear struggling just to survive into middle age. But now, with birth made so much safer and dependable by advances in public health and medical knowledge, I wonder what it would be like if the hundreds of thousands of daily births were to play a larger role in art, philosophy, and religion than the experiences surrounding death and dying in hospital, battlefield, and interstate.

10

Martial Arts

IN 1986, A COLLEAGUE ANDREW SCHMOOKLER wrote a haunting book entitled *The Parable of the Tribes,* which analyzes the dominance of human violence in the shaping of history. The parable is this: let us imagine that eons ago, all of the original tribes of the Earth, save one, were morally opposed to violence. That single other tribe was intent on conquest of others using violent means: then what? The problem he addresses is that a few thugs—religious fanatics, political ideologues, rapacious capitalists—are capable of shaping the world the rest of us have to live in.

Unlike many men, including my own son, I have never had much of a taste for combat. Justifications for the endless cycles of war and political violence have always seemed highly dubious to me. War games never held much interest for me as a boy. When I reached college, I did everything I could to stay out of the military, as did all the other men in my family. As a Jesuit inspired by Daniel Berrigan during Viet Nam, I turned in my draft card, joined the Resistance, and became a counselor to conscientious objectors. None of my cousins have ever entered military service. Nor was there any cult of the warrior in our family, no glorification of war. In fact, all I remember is sadness about its relentless presence, still a muted theme in conversations among my aunts and mother lamenting the various conflicts around the world. The sadness accompanied a deep sense of helplessness, a withering in the face of increasingly powerful forces of militarized political power—all feelings that I inherited.

My mother often says, with a note of resigned weariness, why talk about such things since there's nothing we can do about them.

My grandfather Jul, the only one in our American family who even came close to taking part in a war, is a symbol of the strange identification of manhood with the warrior by men who have never engaged in combat. I have the century-old studio portrait of him outfitted in a Rough Rider uniform for his stint in the Spanish-American War, which used to hang in a prominent place in our house. It is 1898; he is a handsome eighteen-year-old, standing casually cocky, hands clasped in front with his left elbow resting on a straight-backed wicker chair in what looks like a nineteenth-century formal drawing room, wearing a broad brimmed hat, knee-high riding boots, military jacket and riding pants, the cool look of adolescence on his face. Until just recently, I had always believed that he fought in the war, since my father often spoke proudly as if he did. While working on this manuscript, I asked my Aunt Gladys about the details of his military service. With her characteristically ironic smile, she told me that he only got as far as Texas on the train to the front before the war was declared over.

My mother's father, Grandpa Joe, never took part in military service. Even if he had not been over draft age for World War I, I can't imagine him in basic training. He was soft and meek, never did hard physical work nor play sports.

On September 11, 2001, my son Tano was about the same age as I was on December 7, 1941. On that December day, sunny but chilly by California standards, my mother, Grandpa Joe, and I went to the Cathedral as usual for Sunday mass. Because of the cold, we took the streetcar on the way home instead of walking through Capitol Park as we usually did. Just as we were to get off at 19th Street, the conductor announced to everyone that Pearl Harbor

had been bombed and that no one knew whether or not squadrons of Japanese Zeroes were in the air heading on over to bomb us on the mainland.

The details of the day stand out with unusual clarity. We walked the short block from the streetcar stop home and told my dad what had happened before we continued our usual Sunday ritual. After lunch, my dad and I would usually spend the afternoon listening to a series of radio programs—*The Green Hornet, The Shadow, The Jack Benny Program,* and *The George Burns & Gracie Allen Show.* Our radio was an early Magnavox in a walnut cabinet on curved legs high enough off the floor to allow us to lie under the speaker. My dad and I would curl up together close for the afternoon. On that day, Franklin Roosevelt came on to address the nation. His elegant diction and full-bodied resonances, seemingly in full command of the situation, would become for me a source of comfort throughout the years ahead—as it did for others in our neighborhood, which became quiet whenever he addressed the nation, even though we were plagued by terror.

Late in the afternoon on December 7, the three of us went to the old Alhambra Theater and saw Gene Tierney playing Belle Starr, the nineteenth-century feminist outlaw from the old South. Afterwards, we went to the Capitol Tamale Parlor and got take-out. The next morning when I joined other kids walking to Jefferson Elementary School three blocks away, I was struck with fear when I heard them saying that some kamikaze pilots had flown all the way here and might bomb us any day, and that submarines were hovering just off San Francisco and Santa Cruz, waiting to attack.

As the war progressed, cities initiated defense measures. My father was appointed block captain in charge of organizing our neighbors to deal with emergencies in case of attacks. We had sandbags in our house, a bucket for water to extinguish fires, and a shovel for the sand close to the basement door. Periodically, the government would stage mock air raids when sirens would signal the power to the whole city being shut off. B-27s would fly low over us with their bright landing lights tracking over the city, and we would go through the motions of finding shelter in our basement until another round of sirens signaled the end of the exercise.

From then until more than twenty-five years later after the Cuban Missile Crisis, I regularly awoke with a start when a fire engine or ambulance sounded its siren in the night, with a sleep-terror that an air raid was about to happen. Those experiences led me to wonder now what it must be like for generations of Vietnamese or Iraqis who grew up in the midst of real air raids or have endured them their entire lives.

There were many intrusions into everyday life during the war. Chocolate, butter, beef, and mayonnaise disappeared, reserved for the troops overseas. My mother gave me the task of opening Nucoa margarine in big white blocks like lard, and mixing it with yellow coloring in a bowl that I still use. In place of beef, we ate Spam: baked with brown sugar glaze, fried with eggs, in sandwiches, and creamed on toast. Gasoline rationing cut short our long drives. If we ever had to travel after sunset, we were allowed to use only a single small parking light to find our way, with tape over the other. These disturbing changes in our daily lives, though trivial in themselves and nothing compared to what people in other countries were having to deal with, gave me the constant feeling of being in danger beyond the boyish range of my comprehension.

My father was called to the draft. Because of a knee injury from his basketball days, he was classified 4F and given a position as a civilian administrator of the Army Corps of Engineers, charged with supervising the building of military bases throughout Northern California—Camp Beale near Chico, Mather Field and The Signal Corps Depot outside Sacramento, Travis Air Force Base in Fairfield, and Castle Air Force Base in Merced. I looked forward to the ceremonial opening of each new camp when I got to ride in tanks and armored vehicles, and one time even met Governor Earl Warren and played with his children during the afternoon tea party.

We spoke little about my father's first assignment—just that it was to supervise the construction of an internment camp for Japanese-Americans at Tule Lake up near the Oregon border. I remember signs being posted on telephone poles on our block announcing the deportation to this and other camps of our neighbors of Japanese descent, some of whom had been citizens longer than many in our family. They were imprisoned for the duration of the war in that dismal swamp at Tule Lake, searing hot in the summer, disease-making cold in the winter. Some families gave birth to children who decades later became my students. It wasn't until I had driven up to Sacramento to celebrate a Fathers' Day during the 1980s that the topic was ever discussed among us. Congress happened to be in the midst of debating the issuing of monetary reparations for the Japanese-Americans who had lost their homes and businesses during that era, like one of our former neighbors who had been a successful banker. When he returned, aged and visibly broken, he had to eke out a living for his family as a gardener. During our backyard barbecue dinner for Fathers' Day, Aunt Charlotte brought up the topic of the Congressional debate, saying she couldn't understand why they should get anything because it was necessary to imprison them as part of an enemy country. My father agreed saying—I feel impelled to emphasize that I am not exaggerating since it is still hard for me to imagine that he actually would say this—"they had very clean toilets." He kept insisting on this fact, and about how well-designed and neat Tule Lake had been. At first, I couldn't quite believe what I was hearing, thinking maybe that under the influence of a few drinks he was just making offhand remarks, which on reflection would give way to more thoughtful reasons. When I pressed him further, he kept repeating in more detail how well-built and clean the camp was, and that "they" had no reason at all to complain. I argued that our own neighbors were just as American as we, to which he and Charlotte replied that we were at war with "them."

I was barraged with many dark feelings as the argument edged towards violence. On this Fathers' Day, I felt deeply ashamed of my father. I saw him as similar to the fathers of Germans I knew of my generation, upstanding Christian citizens who had capitulated to Hitler simply because he was in a position of authority, not daring to risk the consequences of following their consciences. I was furious at him for insisting on the defense of what seemed to me to be an outrageously immoral policy; I would have given anything to hear him simply apologize with the understandable acknowledgement that now, knowing better, he regretted what had happened. In addition to being enraged, I was also humiliated at how pathetic he seemed in using the rationale of clean toilets and neatly designed concrete buildings to justify ruining the lives of American families who were immigrants like our own family. This was my heritage as a man, a moral impotence making it difficult for me to implement what I believed was right. I left Sacramento that night not knowing if my father and I would ever be able to speak to each other again.

As I explored the climate of denial among our family about the war as I was working on this book, I asked my mother, nearing a hundred years old, if she remembered knowing about the Holocaust before the end of the war. "No," she said, "we were so far away from everything, it wasn't until after the war when Life brought out the photos of the camps that I found out about it."

Although I grew up as a boy among fears of the fantasized dangers about us from Japan and Germany, my mental grasp of this and other wars came from novels, Christian theology, and Hollywood movies. Elementary school history was a sanitized abstract of battles between heroic good guys and very strong bad guys. We rejoiced when we heard of some progress on our side, with no sense of what the course of war was doing to children like myself.

In the late afternoon of August 5, 1945, Glenn Freitas, my closest neighbor friend, and I were sitting on the corner of 19th and N Streets. In those days, papers were still hawked throughout the city by boys walking around yelling out the headlines.

Extra! Extra! Read All About It!
Atom Bomb destroys Japanese City!

I remember the joy of that moment, relieved that the War was nearly over and we could once again have chocolate and butter. When I saw the photos of the great mushroom cloud, I felt such exhilaration at the grandeur of it all, proud that our side had managed to create such a glorious object of annihilation. Nagasaki deepened my pride and sense of relief that my country was strong enough to fend off anyone who might endanger my life. The photos, of course, were all from a great distance, showing none of the human horror at the ground level.

The Bomb became the icon of my pubescence. Its strength was so magnificent that we could see its radiance in the night sky whenever it was exploded in tests at Yucca Flats some three hundred miles south in the Mojave Desert outside Las Vegas. Not many years later, I would be envious of Joan Didion, who got permission as a journalist to witness the test explosions close up. Of all these cosmic blasts, the most gorgeous and awe-inspiring were the tests of Edward "Strangelove" Teller's new H-Bomb at Bikini: grand columns of water and smoke erupting into the stratosphere, a secular apocalypse proving that we indeed were strong and safe from the likes of Tojo, Hitler, Mussolini, and Stalin.

Entering adolescence, I had not the least sense of the horrible carnages that war wreaks on ordinary families—not only the physical

rippings of flesh and killings, but the destruction of homes and cultivated lands, the displacement of whole cultures from one region of
the world to another. I had no idea of Hitler's systematic slaughters
of Jews, gypsies, Blacks, and gays; nor that Stalin and Mao were
well along the way to accomplishing purges beyond imagination in
scope. I wonder now what my teachers—public grade-school teachers, the nuns, priests, and Christian Brothers in middle- and high-
school—were thinking when they failed to speak with us about these
events that were radically changing the worlds we were about to
inherit. As far as I can recall, "history" began with Alexander the
Great and never got any further than Grant and Lee at Appomat-
tox. I can only guess that my teachers, like my family, were relieved
to find themselves in a quiet place hoping to be protected from
such horrors. What would be the point of disturbing it?

The closest I ever got to war was two years in the ROTC, required
of all freshmen and sophomores at the University of Santa Clara.
The bi-weekly class lectures were read verbatim from a standard text
by a drill sergeant—like many of the men I worked with during the
summers on construction jobs with my father, he was a beefy man
with little education who clearly resented smart-assed college kids.
He showed films of soldiers with bloody wounds from shrapnel designed to give us a sense of the seriousness and glory of fighting for
our country. Lurid films of syphilitic lesions warned us of the dangers
of going to prostitutes during our missions overseas, a fear that was
already instilled in my by the priests and Christian Brothers.

I felt oddly nervous and clumsy during the weekly close-order
drill in full uniform with rifles. I couldn't get the steps right, just
as I couldn't get ballroom dance steps right; I kept dropping my
rifle during the presenting of arms and turning the wrong way at
a command of a fancy move. At the end of our sophomore year,

we had the option to continue ROTC with the requirement of four years of service after college as officers in return for a substantial stipend towards tuition. The Korean War was in progress, the likely assignment for any who volunteered for this program. Only two of the 150 classmates chose to drop out. My friend did so for anti-war philosophical reasons, about which he has been an articulate spokesman ever since. I was motivated mostly by feeling incompetent at drill and shooting, and by fear of battle. I went to some lengths to gain a 4F draft status for asthma, which by then had in fact abated enough to let me serve had I been pressured.

The hermetic era of the Sacramento of my boyhood, with its seeming insulation from worldly violence, came to an end. Anthony Swofford, another Sacramento boy two generations younger than I, has written a testosterone-rich memoir of his stint as a Marine in the Gulf War (*Jarhead,* now a film), which dramatizes the change in our hometown. He grew up in an army family in the post-war suburbs near McClellan Field and entered the Marines when he was just out of high school. His account has two plots. One is of sweaty male camaraderie nurtured by boot-camp face-punching, communal butt-fucking, shared whoring, pornography in the barracks, drunkenness, and endurance contests. The other story is of a vague war going on in which he is trained as an advanced sharpshooter to kill people for reasons that neither he nor his friends have any knowledge about, nor even care to know.

I feel both a revulsion for the manhood he describes as well as a certain regret at never having belonged to it, a fraternity I looked at from afar as they played sports, wrestled on the lawns, felt up girls, drove souped-up vehicles way beyond safe speeds, shot ducks and deer, and eventually the enemy. They seemed to enjoy a muscular community of intimate friendships that lasted for life, unlike myself who can count only a handful of life-long male friends. The long-ing is due in part to my early twentieth-century California isolation from the realities of fleshy violence, which Swofford lays bare for all non-militants to see, stripped of those delusions of patriotic gran-deur, which my Grandfather Jul embraced in his Spanish-American War regalia. And yet, at the same time, it is a longing for a vigorous strength, raring to charge into life full-bore, for which I've had to reach only with great difficulty over the years so that I might get off the bed of my antihistaminic stupors and despair to engage in creating a more humane world.

It was not until my mid-forties that I ventured outside the United States, except for brief trips to Mexico. By the time of my first trip to Europe, although I had been thoroughly educated in world his-tory, both by my own reading and graduate school education, I hadn't realized how protected my sensibilities had been from the constant presence of violence in the lives of such a large percent-age of human beings. When I was living and working in Paris and traveling throughout the region, I would be strolling down a street in old Paris glowing after a sensual lunch and suddenly find myself in front of a plaque on the wall of a school that told about Jewish children who had been deported from there to the camps during the War. On my first trip to Venice, I was finding my way through the ancient passageways and canals when I chanced upon what I discovered was the original Ghetto, with a list of those who had died in the camps. Each quaint village of Normandy and Provence had prominent remembrances of the young men who died in the two World Wars. Everywhere the scars of war, among every family, every late-night conversation.

My German and Austrian students often reveal a haunting de-spair about the world, raised by parents who had done something to survive during the Hitler years, but would not say what it was. Their pessimism was so severe that few were willing to risk bring-ing children into a world that they felt was growing steadily more dangerous. I saw the intellectual heritage of Europe, in which I had been steeped, in a new light—how deeply the chain of large and small wars had impacted literature, painting, music, and dance, as well as the seemingly more abstract questions of philosophy. From that time on, as I traveled from one country to another, my ab-stract schema of history became progressively colored in with one carnage after another, becoming more like Goya's etchings than a Norman Rockwell cover for the *Saturday Evening Post*.

In 1996, I was spending a month with my wife and son in a small medieval village between the French Pyrenees and Toulouse near Albi, where a friend had offered us his villa. In high school many years earlier, I had studied the savage wars the Popes waged in this region against the so-called Albigensian heretics and the Cathars in the twelfth and thirteenth centuries, but my knowledge was ethere-al, remaining in some remote file of my brain with no impact on my feelings about life. The villa's library contained a number of books on these communities, careful studies coming out of a renewed in-terest of scholars in this period. The Cathars were akin to modern evangelical churches, loosely organized, strung out among the small villages of what is still a largely unpopulated region of France, with-out a formal priesthood and centrally established bodies of dogma. What disturbed the Parisians and the Romans were the anti-author-itarian beliefs of the villagers. Craftsmen sharing their products, they espoused early versions of socialist economies, refusing to give portions of their labor over to absent feudal lords. I learned that Simon de Montfort, the Pope's general, had spent ten years trying to assault two of the last remaining villages of the network, Queribus and Peyrepetus, until his armies managed to slaughter every man, woman, and child. One day as we were driving through the hills we suddenly came upon stunning views of each of these villages, high on jagged mountains, their ruins white in the Occitan sun. I was gripped by a soul-shaking understanding of how bloodthirsty must have been the religious zeal of popes, theologians, nobles, and bootsoldiers that they would endure such difficulties for so long in pursuit of this vicious mission.

After the final victory of the papal army, the Cardinal delegated by the Pope to oversee the slaughter was then assigned to make the short journey over the Pyrenees to assume the role of the first Spanish Inquisitor General. At the same time, the Crusades were in full swing not far to the East, with its armies of Christian heroes setting out to slaughter darker-hued men, women, and children named "infidels." In response, a new militaristic sect of Shiite Islam was formed, the *Hashsashin*, Assassins, using hashish to stoke up their attacks on the Christian plunderers.

One night my wife and I were walking the streets of an Italian village, strangely quiet. Passing cafés with the televisions blaring, I realized that it was a European League championship soccer game, with Liverpool playing Milan. We entered a trattoria. As we ate our pasta, a strange scene was happening on the screen, narrated in Italian, which neither of us understood. Men were streaming onto the playing field wielding pieces of lumber, beating each other. It was only by scanning the next day's *International Herald Tribune* that I realized we had witnessed the largest ever of the many soccer massacres, in which more than three hundred people died in a bloody fight between the British and the Italian spectators, leaving the stands ripped to shreds. A strange new thought came to me: this is not a primitive bestial act but one of a highly advanced culture. Things seemed to be getting worse, I thought to myself, not better as my hopes would have it.

✧

Even now, however, there is a radical difference in the kind of awareness of war's omnipresence that one finds in Sacramento in contrast to places like Paris, Moscow, or Taipei, a difference that partly accounts for our narcissistic national politics. In other parts of the world, people have realistic fears about the terrors of war and their causes. In Sacramento, there is an aura of free-floating fear, unrooted in present or historical fact. It is like the fear I felt for many decades beginning in late 1941 when I was always alert to the possibility that Japanese suicide bombers might be on their way to kill us—or later, that nuclear missiles might be in the air while I slept. That kind of fear makes people easily fall victim to rumor, innuendo, and ultimately to political manipulation. It is a chronically irrational state, dissociated from immediate experience and lacking an intelligence capable of sensible analysis of objectively dangerous situations.

11

Salmon in the Shadows

Revisioning as I have experienced it is not a luxury but life itself, a matter of survival; trying to stay alive in history; improvising a raft after shipwreck, out of whatever materials are available. Out of whatever materials are available: bits of books, the fragments we shore up against our ruin.[20]

—Norman O. Brown, *Apocalypse and/or Metamorphosis*

Such is this book: a gathering of what I have available to keep hope alive, struggling to give an authentic answer to Jason's question about my third wish: what kinds of hope have tough enough fibers to sustain the inevitable pressures of personal failure and social collapse?

The yawning Sacramento Valley was one of the first true experiments in the egalitarian dream of America as a melting pot of cultures. From the first months of the Gold Rush, it has been populated by immigrant Chinese, Armenians, Mexicans, Portuguese, Japanese, Filipino, Scandinavian, and Swiss, who were drawn there for different reasons, but neither as imperial colonialists nor as refugees from religious persecution. Most came in severe poverty; many came in conditions of slave labor, brought in to service the mines, the Union Pacific Railroad, the orchards and farms, and finally the

✧ 163

vast post-war webs of pipelines and freeways. They were people desperate for jobs, hoping for a golden future.

As my mother was entering her nineties, a young couple bought the house next door to hers. They were young lawyers: he, Jewish, member of the local synagogue; she, a Korean immigrant. They soon made old-fashioned neighborly gestures, bringing her fresh-baked cookies, extra food from a big meal, inviting her to movies, even to the local baseball games. In her ninety years, the only Jews to have been hosted in my mother's home were my first wife and her family. The only non-white was the single visit of an African-American secretary of my college friend John Vasconcellos. Other than that, she had only rare social contacts with non-Whites or non-Christians, especially in her home. Now, at this late age, she found herself welcomed into their family and social gatherings where, she reported, she was the only Wonder-Bread white person without an advanced college degree among a mixture of Mexican-, African-, and Asian-Americans.

What struck me about her reports was her repeating how comfortable she felt there, warmly received, asked for her opinions, respected for her age—not like the isolation she says, with a certain edge, that she often feels among my friends. It occurred to me that it was not accidental that these people were not the familiar upwardly mobile white Christians of my parents' world; they were more like the immigrants of my great-grandparents' and grandparents' era, somehow having a friendly awareness that the neighbors, like themselves, no matter what their religion or color, had worked very hard to escape from somewhere to get here, and were serious about working together to shape a better life for their children. They knew enough about life and history to recognize that building relations with one's neighbors and cultivating kindness were more crucial in shaping that better life than any abstract ideologies, no matter how enlightened. They also carried an Old-World respect for elders, which has long been lost in our youth-oriented culture.

My mother's experience is evidence of the many very small ways in which the unformed dreams of the first settlers in Sacramento have been realized. The city has evolved into a comfortable and humane place for the patchwork collection of people from many other places who can live here more easily than their forbears were able to live in many of the worlds from which they came.

It ranks sixth in the country for diversity, just behind Houston, Los Angeles, and New York. That ranking was calculated from the odds that any two residents, chosen at random, will be of different races or ethnicities. It predicts how often the next person you meet walking down the street will be different from you. Its elected officials—local, state, and federal—transgress the old-fashioned barriers of gender and ethnic background, men and women, Hispanic, Asian, African, Buddhist, Catholic, Atheist.

Sacramento hovers around fifteenth in the country for its economy, rated according to number of jobs, wages, and diversity of economy (state government, universities, large and small businesses, construction). There are more than a hundred miles of biking and walking trails bordering the American and Sacramento Rivers. With the end of the Cold War, the military sprawls surrounding the city—Mather and McClellan Fields, the Signal Depot, and Aerojet—were closed, thereby leaving vast spaces for imaginative new urban designs. The city was the first to vote in favor of decommissioning its nuclear power plant because of a widely shared unwillingness to risk unknown dangers of radiation for the sake of more efficient electricity generation.

On the months of warm nights that grace the city, one has the choice of many outdoor cafés with good food and music. Both at the Convention Center and the Mondavi Center fifteen minutes away in Davis, one finds all the cutting-edge music, dance, and drama that are on the circuit from Brooklyn to Minneapolis and San Francisco. The light rail system is slowly making its way throughout the vast suburbs, a model for other cities. Easy drives give access to a limitless range of outdoor recreation in the Sierras, the Trinity Alps, Shasta and Lassen, the Monterey Bay, in addition to the many channels of the Delta and the river forks of the foothills.

But the very success of the city puts into greater relief its challenges. When I was growing up, the population hovered around 100,000; as of the 2000 census, it is 1.2 million. The pleasure of the outdoor café and backyard life are marred by the omnipresent roar of interstates that lace the city, augmented by leaf-blowers and jet transports. The traffic is thick with people coming and going from the sprawl of suburbs that keep inching up towards Auburn and Placerville in the Mother Lode, and down towards Lodi and Stockton. The thoroughfares are clogged a good part of the day, with Sacramento ranking fifteenth in the nation for the number of hours the average person spends in traffic. The air is so polluted that on many days children and the old are encouraged to remain indoors. Fresno, just a couple of hours down Highway 99, has the most polluted air and the highest rate of childhood asthma in the United States.

Tucked up against the old levees and out in the diked-up floodplains are the growing tracts of the poor, the drug-traffickers, the drive-by shooters, who make Sacramento one of the most unsafe places to live in the United States. Gang violence is rampant. The ubiquitous armored screen doors on the houses with conspicuous notices of alarm systems are reminders that this seemingly safe haven has higher rates of murder, theft, and hit-and-run accidents than New York or Los Angeles. It ranks fifth in the United States for the percentage of cars per capita stolen every year. Every house in my mother's tree-lined, lawn-carpeted, tranquil, upscale neighborhood, including her own, has been broken into and burglarized. Several of her friends have been mugged in daylight, or had their cars stolen or vandalized. The nearby synagogue was recently bombed, destroying its library of priceless old texts. It was eventually discovered that the culprits were two devotees of the Aryan Brotherhood from the northern reaches of the Valley who previously had been convicted of rape and murder.

The rivers are so polluted that no one can eat the fish nor allow themselves to swallow the water when they are swimming. The alluvial soils have been saturated with chemicals over the past century, and by poisons from the military bases.

Gold Rush immigrants to the great Central Valley of California like my uncles Andy and Charley and great-grandmother Lucy were caught between two seemingly different possibilities of shaping this new world. The more visionary plan would require complex strategies of how to join peacefully with the first settlers—the Miwok, Maidu, Patwin, and Yokuts—to marry the land in respect and skill, cultivating the unimaginably prolific bottomland watered by the Sacramento, Yuba, American, Tuolumne, Merced, and San Joaquin Rivers, more than enough for everyone, creating a Utopia the likes of which had not been known since Ur of the Chaldees, centuries before the fertile Tigris and Euphrates Garden of Eden suffered its devastations by oil rigs, land mines, and smart bombs.

Visionary choices in those early decades demanded more extensive stores of imagination than could be expected from people who had to give all their attention to survival. Except for the Chinese, Japanese, and a handful of Jewish families, the settlers were rarely people with much education beyond the basics. Unlike the Eastern seaboard and the deep South, the Valley carried few residues of the religion, laws, medicines, and class structures of England, Holland, and France. By contrast to the intimate estuaries and canyons of the Pacific coast, the Central Valley was little affected by the

Spanish missions of Junipero Serra and his Franciscans, or by the organizations of the vast land grants, which would become the new cities and suburbs with Spanish names and Old World Catholic hierarchies in the governing of San Francisco, Santa Barbara, and Nuestra Señora de Los Angeles. For my great-grandparents and grandparents—if not for the Indians who had lived there forever—it appeared to be an unformed New World, lying in a state of nature waiting to be shaped, it was erroneously thought, by pioneers who considered themselves unencumbered by history, literature and philosophy, of which most of them were ignorant.

Like many of Sacramento's early settlers, my relatives came there desperately poor. Still reeling from the long journeys they took to get here, they needed to eke out a new existence for themselves and their young children as fast as they could. From meagre financial and emotional resources, they managed to create a long healthy humane life for themselves and their offspring. Their interests were building houses, growing vegetables, flower gardens, chickens, and watching their children and grandchildren grow into adulthoods with new hopes. They worked hard so that my cousins and I could be the first in our lineage to attend college. My mother and my father's sisters still carry on, now approaching a hundred, independent, having made it clear to us all that they want to remain in their homes to the very end. Their aspirations are modest: enjoyment of the unfolding lives of their children and grandchildren, good food, frequent gatherings with their friends, an occasional trip to faraway places.

More visionary hopes flicker among my relatives quietly in the shadows of their modest lives. My mother frequently expresses sadness over the continued cycles of war, violence, and greed, and her disgust about the hypocrisies of politics. Her laments reflect her lifetime immersion in the Bible with its insistence on generous caring for other people, especially those most in need no matter

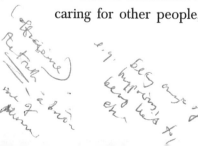

what their religious beliefs or cultural heritage, and on its repetitive proscriptions of violence.

Everywhere around me there seem to have been people hoping to find a viable way of bringing together mundane earthly hopes for a more comfortable personal and family life with soulful visions of a more humane social order. Achieving that integration has been a difficult and frustrating struggle in the face of the tenacious greed that has transformed the Valley into the most lucrative land venture ever imagined. Miners sluiced out every precious metal and mineral from the foothills. Brokers crazed the once-soft topsoil with a lacework of freeways, parceled out the depleted land for real estate, cornered the market on the vast water sources, cut up huge tracts for The Southern and Northern Pacific railroads to bring in the purchasers and the workers, powered by the Pacific Gas and Electric Company, with the old farming towns eventually becoming the bedrooms for lower-income employees in the San Francisco Bay metropolis. The efforts of religious and secular idealists to turn back the tides of greed are so fragmented, one community from another, that they achieve only the smallest measures of success.

✧

Less than a mile from my current house just north of San Francisco is a small stream which begins up on Mount Tamalpais and swells with other streams as it plunges down a ravine into the ancient redwoods of Muir Woods, where it forms Redwood Creek and meanders a short two miles out to the sea. Decades ago, the salmon stopped their yearly spawning run up the creek when it became clogged with debris and the intrusions of imported plants. Residents of our small watershed got together and cleaned the creek over a period of a couple of years. Then, just recently, the salmon returned. Around each new year, you can see these long colorful fish hovering under the bridges quietly spawning their eggs.

When I saw the first group of those returning refugees, my heart awakened with a kind of hope I have only rarely touched upon. There was little reason to justify it in the face of the seemingly invincible dark forces of nature-polluting corporate greed, partisan politics, terrorism, and spiritual hypocrisy. And yet, I felt a sense of expectation more ancient in vigor and the wisdom of survival than any fragile humanly-constructed hope.

As I keep learning more about Africa, the Middle East, Southeast Asia, Australia, Hawaii, and the very land on which I am living—everywhere violence, mass slaughter, and forced displacement of populations from their homes—I puzzle about what can withstand such storms. Against their tsunami turbulence, hopes based on a few salmon reappearing in Redwood Creek can seem like yet another California pollyanna dream, a dance against Death. Yet, something seems to lurk there in the depths. Like those Rembrandt paintings where the thick smears of black pigments cover most of the surfaces, making the few hints of yellows and reds on the cheeks of his self-portrait, or the naked body of the infant Jesus, or the blush of Susanna attacked by the elders, give off an even deeper radiance than if they sat there muddled in with other bright colors.

Notes

1. W. G. Sebald, "An Attempt at Restitution," in *Campo Santo,* trans. Anthea Bell (New York: Modern Library, 2006), p. 202.

2. Joan Didion, *Where I Was From* (New York: Knopf, 2003), p. 38.

3. Richard Rodriguez, *Brown: The Last Discovery of America* (New York: Viking Penguin, 2002), p. 171.

4. F. M. Alexander, "After the Bomb," in *The Resurrection of the Body* (New York: Dell, 1969), pp. 87ff.

5. Rodriguez, *op. cit.,* p. 113.

6. "Land of the Mean, Home of the Rage," *The San Francisco Chronicle,* Wednesday, April 3, 2002, p. 2.

7. Wilhelm Reich, *The Mass Psychology of Fascism,* trans. Vincent Carafagno (New York: Farrar, Straus & Giroux, 1970), p. 47.

8. *Ibid.,* p. 69.

9. Pierre Bourdieu, *Distinction: A Social Critique of the Judgment of Taste,* trans. Richard Nice (Cambridge, MA: Harvard, 1984), p. 196.

10. Norbert Elias, *The History of Manners: The Civilizing Process,* Volume I, trans. Edmund Jephcott (New York: Pantheon, 1978), p. 262.

11. "The Penitential of Cummean," II, 6, *The Irish Penitentials,* ed. Ludwig Bieler (Oxford: Oxford University Press, 1963).

12. *Loc. cit.*

13. Fr. Heribert Jone, *Moral Theology,* Englished and Adapted to the Laws and Customs of the United States of America, trans. and adapted by Fr. Urban Adelman (Westminster, MD: Newman Press, 1963), p. 228.

14. Mary Karr, "What Do I Do for an Encore?" symposium, *Author's Guild Bulletin,* Summer 2001, p. 33.

15. *San Francisco Chronicle,* October 20, 2004, p. B5.

16. Elizabeth Beringer, "Interview with Ilse Middendorf," in *Bone, Breath, and Gesture,* ed. Don Hanlon Johnson (Berkeley, CA: North Atlantic Books, 1995), pp. 68, 69.

17. *Op. cit.,* p. 71.

18. *The Spiritual Exercises of St. Ignatius,* trans. Louis Puhl, S.J. (Westminster, MD: The Newman Press, 1960), pp. 32, 33.

19. Jane Butterfield English, *A Different Doorway: Adventures of a Caesarean Born* (Pt. Reyes Station, CA: Earth Heart Press, 1985).

20. Norman O. Brown, *Apocalypse and/or Metamorphosis* (Berkeley: UC Press, 1991), p. 158.

Acknowledgments

Barbara Holifield, a Jungian analyst and my wife, has played a major role in the shaping of this text, having contributed thoughtful and often challenging feedback as I developed it. My son Tano has been a constant inspiration with his vitality, wit, and evocative questions. The lively dialogue portrayed in this book among him and his friends Jason Stern and Ian Martin was a key event in helping me organize many of the fragments that had not yet come together around a single theme. Listening in to the constant banter of these and other friends has helped me get a feel for the emerging shapes of fresh visions for the world instead of sinking into an elder's nostalgia for the past.

During the twenty years since my father and uncles died, I have found myself listening intently to ongoing conversations among my mother and my aunts Gladys and Charlotte, peppered with irony and humor, about details of the past. Living more among reveries of the past than in the roiling present, as one would expect of women approaching one hundred years of age, they embody a history of the Sacramento Valley in the twentieth century. The three of them rarely agree about the details of any particular event, and are often united in disputing my memory, thus prodding me into deeper investigations of what actually happened.

My writing partners Susan Griffin, Bokara Legendre, and Daidie Donnelly have given me a wealth of feedback and encouragement both about the craft of writing and about how to negotiate the rocky shoals of the industry. Other helpers along the way include Marty Krasny, Bruce Baker, Nina Wise, Haru Murakawa, Ron Scapp, Jay Ogilvy, Betsy Behnke, Michael Marsh, Corey Fisher, Pall and Jennifer Walton, China Galland, and Gene Gendlin.

My students at the California Institute of Integral Studies are an ongoing source of fresh thinking and new images. Their responses to my writing over the years have been like the tides moving the sands, an everyday presence that shapes me almost without my noticing. When I do stop and take account, I find how much they have affected me. In particular, I am indebted to David Ruettiger for his help in marketing the book; also, to Ian Grand, old friend and chair of the Somatics Psychology Program at CIIS, who has warmly supported my writing as an integral part of my contribution to the program.

Over the years, I have been touched by the appreciation for my work shown by North Atlantic's founder and author Richard Grossinger, with whom I share so many basic and somewhat quirky views about the state of things. In addition, the team that he assigned to publish the book—editor Yvonne Cárdenas, publicist Debbie Matsumoto, copyeditor Kathy Glass, designers Susan Quasha and Paula Morrison, sales & marketing associate Saudah Mirza—represent an older era of publishing motivated at least as much by aesthetics and meaning as by bottom-line calculations.

About the Author

Don Hanlon Johnson is a professor of Somatics at The California Institute of Integral Studies in the School of Professional Psychology, in San Francisco, California. He holds a PhD in philosophy from Yale University and an MA in theology. Having begun his career teaching academic philosophy, Johnson shifted to practical studies of various methods of deepening body experience and changing body structure. After studying with Dr. Ida Rolf for eight years, he authored the first book on rolfing, *The Protean Body.*

Johnson's professional specialty is the field of Somatics, which he helped to create. It represents an integration of a wide range of body practices that pose an effective challenge to harmful assumptions that currently shape medicine, education, and religion. He has taught throughout Europe and in Taiwan and Japan, and now teaches an annual course at Ritsumeikan University in Kyoto on the relation between body practices and human services. He is also a contributing editor of the professional journal *Somatics.*

For several years, Johnson organized joint projects between leaders of major religious institutions and leaders of various schools of Somatics in the U.S. and in Russia. One of the results of those seminars was the creation of a healing center for survivors of political torture, which is now doing work in connection with Survivors International. Johnson has also been a participant in a variety of projects whose aim is to restore a sense of the importance of human experience in a non-authoritarian context.

Over the past forty years, Johnson has published six books and countless articles. From the time of his first publications, he has cultivated an approach to non-fiction writing that grounds theory in narrative material.

Johnson's expertise in the body of *Everyday Hopes, Utopian Dreams*—twentieth-century Sacramento—comes from having been born there to a pioneering family; working as a young man with his grandfather and father who built many of the original houses in the city, and in working on construction of some of the major buildings and thoroughfares; and growing up among contemporaries like Joan Didion and Richard Rodriguez who saw the home-world as a fertile source of insights about how to write into America itself.

His expertise in the soul of the book, which is philosophical and theological, comes from his education and professional life. He has engaged in the philosophical work of making sense of the world in those areas where sense seems absent. He has given special attention to the harmful effects of mind-body dualism in the West—on education, psychology, religion, medicine, and politics. His work has focused on social transformation through the lens of healing practices, the nature of the human body, and the structures of human communication. He has long been active in bringing together people from a wide variety of theoretical and practical viewpoints, and ethnic backgrounds with the aim of initiating greater cooperation in addressing critical problems facing us at this period in history. Writing has been a central part of this work: striving to recover the frail connections between word and flesh.

[handwritten notes:]

020 Dardebro

762988888

fnw1001@cam.ac.uk

roger.trigg@theology.ox.ac.uk

justin.barrett@anthro.ox.ac.uk